SPACE
AND
SOCIETY

*Studies for the Seminar on Problems of Outer Space
sponsored by the
Carnegie Endowment for International Peace*

EDITED BY
HOWARD J. TAUBENFELD

1964
Oceana Publications, Inc.
Dobbs Ferry, New York

PRINTED IN U.S.A.   ALPERT PRESS, INC., Brooklyn, N. Y.

For Rita, David and Marc

For Rita, David and Marc

Editor's Foreword

In an effort to provide a setting in which at least a limited number of people with a direct interest and concern in the implications of space activities could get together informally to exchange views, the Carnegie Endowment for International Peace sponsored a seminar series on outer space problems in New York City in the spring of 1963. Members of the seminar, not all of whom were present at each session, included Dr. Robert Barre, Scientist for Social, Economic and Political Studies, N.A.S.A.; Professor DeForest Billyou, New York University Law School; Professor Richard Falk, Princeton University; Miss J. A. C. Gutteridge, Counsellor, United Kingdom Mission to the United Nations; Dr. Robert Jastrow, Director, N.A.S.A. Institute for Space Studies; John Johnson, Esq., then General Counsel, N.A.S.A.; Arthur Levine, N.A.S.A. Institute for Space Studies; Professor Myres McDougal, Yale Law School; Horace P. Moulton, Esq., Vice-President and General Counsel, A. T. & T.; Leonard Silk, Editor, *Business Week;* Oscar Schachter, Esq., Director, General Legal Division, United Nations; Sanford Schwarz, Esq., United Nations; Professor Robert Woetzel, New York and Fordham Universities; Christopher Wright, Director, Columbia University Council for Atomic Age Studies, and the undersigned. Present from the Carnegie Endowment were Francis Deak, Lawrence S. Finkelstein and E. Raymond Platig, Robert Bloom, Esq., and Cecil W. Boodey, Jr., served as rapporteurs.

For eight of the nine sessions, a member of the seminar led the discussion and in six instances, a paper was circulated in advance. Those papers, modified and revised, form the heart of this book. Of course, they represent only the views of the authors—discussions in the seminar usually revealed divergent and strongly held views on most issues. In some instances, the papers have appeared in different form in other publications, and where essential, permission to use has been graciously granted. My wife, Rita Falk Taubenfeld, and I have added an introductory chapter giving an overview of what we feel are the most vital problem areas needing national attention. In addition, Dr. Platig has most helpfully drawn on the six papers presented at the seminar, the discussions and his own erudition to open more widely some of the questions merely touched on or suggested, to put some questions in different context, to raise some new questions, to suggest some unarticulated relationships between the papers and, in his own words, "to provide a layman's expression of the current state of his understanding and wonderment." Messrs. McDougal and Schwarz did not circulate papers in advance of the discussions they led on liability problems and on the use of international organizations in outer space matters, respectively. Professor McDougal's views can be found in the recently published book by McDougal, Lasswell and Vlasic, *Law and Public Order in Space* (1963).

My heartfelt thanks go to all participants in the seminar, and especially to those members who accepted the role of discussion leader for making the sessions a stimulating intellectual exercise. Our rapporteurs, Messrs. Bloom and Boodey made a real contribution through excellent, rapidly available reports on talks and discussion at each meeting. Special thanks are also due my wife for her contribution to Chapter 7. The thanks of all of the participants go to the Carnegie Endowment for sponsoring the meetings, and for providing essential administrative and secretarial assistance. This seminar on problems of outer space is but one of many personally rewarding activities made possible for me by my designation as Visiting Research Scholar at the Endowment in 1962-63 for which I am deeply grateful. It is my hope that this little volume may stimulate further thought on problems already apparent in keeping man's increasing outer space activities both peaceful and beneficial not only to the national interest, but to the well-being of all mankind.

HOWARD J. TAUBENFELD

Table of Contents

Contributors

RICHARD A. FALK   *Professor,* Princeton University

ROBERT JASTROW   *Director,* Goddard Institute for Space Studies, N.A.S.A.

HORACE P. MOULTON   *Vice President and General Counsel,* American Telephone and Telegraph Company

E. RAYMOND PLATIG   *Director of Studies,* Carnegie Endowment for International Peace

LEONARD SILK   *Senior Editor and Economist, Business Week*

RITA F. TAUBENFELD   *Economic Analyst*

HOWARD J. TAUBENFELD   *Professor of Law,* Southern Methodist University

ROBERT K. WOETZEL   *Professor* at New York and Fordham Universities

Introduction

This collection, which its inspirer and editor terms a "little volume," is a welcome bonus from the year Professor Taubenfeld spent as the Carnegie Endowment Visiting Research Scholar. That Scholarship is offered on terms that permit the incumbent virtually complete discretion as to how he will use his time and exploit his freedom from normal burdens and responsibilities. The only important qualification is that, however the time be used, it be used for the most part with us, in the Carnegie Endowment's New York headquarters, so that my colleagues and I may have the stimulating, sometimes provoking, benefit of a "thinker in residence." Professor Taubenfeld served us well in this respect. In addition, however, he contributed vigorously during the year to the several intellectual communities to which he belongs. Among those contributions is this collection, stemming from the seminar series that was organized on Professor Taubenfeld's initiative and led by him. The Carnegie Endowment is grateful to him and to his collaborators in the enterprise for their role in making the book possible.

One theme that may be said to dominate the book — as it dominates man's space venture — is the mutual impact of man in space and man on earth. To what extent does space pose problems and challenges which are essentially new to man? To what extent is space no more than an arena in which man's traditional values and behavior patterns are projected? Some years ago, in my introduction to the Report of the Carnegie Endowment for 1956-57, written in the wake of Sputnik's electrifying orbit, I said: "Although recent events have added grim new dimensions to the business of foreign policy, the old problems of war and peace are still with us, and have not essentially changed. The field has been enlarged, to be sure. The stakes mount ever higher. But despite the breakthrough into space, the main elements are essentially unchanged: men's beliefs, fears, and desires, the balances in the power they control, the issues and bits of ground over which they contest, the restraints on their conduct that they accept or that are imposed on them. . . ."

Clearly, man's character has not changed just because he has the developing capacity to intrude on the heavens. Nor has space, — whether it is viewed as a field for competition, as an opportunity for cooperation, or as a resource for exploitation, — yet given any signs of substantially altering the by-now familiar patterns of competition, cooperation, and exploitation on earth. Thus far, the limited experience we have leads to two hypotheses: that the powers with space capabilities view space primarily as another medium in which to pursue national interests and policies and in which to confront essentially familiar problems, and that they are unlikely to deny themselves such national advantage as competition may appear to offer. None of the authors in this volume disagrees with these general hypotheses, although several of the authors offer thoughts on advancing beyond them.

However, these generalizations should not go without qualification. There are at least three respects in which countervailing considerations exist which might over time assume increasing importance.

In the first place, there is the large, as yet virtually unexamined, question of what knowledge about the universe may imply for knowledge of ourselves. No one who reads Robert Jastrow's brief but vibrant and dramatic description of what we may learn from space can fail to be deeply impressed by the knowledge space may have to offer, not only about the physical character of the universe and about our physical environment on earth but, beyond both of these, about our concept of ourselves in relation to our earth and of its relation to that larger universe the outer edge of which we are barely beginning to explore.

Some years ago, the imagination of the press and public was captured by the suggestion that intelligent life might be discovered in this or another solar system. Clearly, one cannot exclude the possibility that life exists and will be discovered in space. The philosophical implications of such a discovery would be profound. However, it is not necessary to assume such a discovery in order to be aware that our enlarging knowledge of space is likely to have important impacts on our understanding of ourselves. Indeed, history points us to this insight. Even without physical intrusion from earth, space has already profoundly influenced not only our understanding of our physical environment but our metaphysical outlook as well. Ptolemy, Copernicus and Galileo are witnesses to that. Looking to the future, I am reminded of Sir Charles Oman's observation, quoted by Professor Samuel Eliot Morison in his biography of Christopher Columbus, about the impact on European thought of Columbus' voyage of discovery to the New World: "A new envisagement of the world has begun, and men are no longer sighing after the imaginary golden age that lay in the distant past but speculating as to the golden age that might possibly lie in the on-coming future." [1] Do we stand on the verge of a similar intellectual and philosophical invigoration? Professor Jastrow's contribution to this volume suggests that we may.

Secondly, there is recent evidence of growing awareness that the space adventure does involve the kind of calculus of gains and costs outlined by Leonard Silk in his thoughtful essay in this volume. That calculus involves not only the direct ratio between the benefits to be derived from space

---

[1] Sir Charles Oman, *On the Writing of History*, 1939, (New York: E. P. Dutton and Company), p. 117, quoted by Samuel Eliot Morison, *Admiral of the Ocean Sea*, (Boston: Little, Brown), 1942, p. 5.

exploration and the costs of undertaking such exploration, but also the comparison between this use of resources and other national scientific efforts. My colleague, Dr. E. Raymond Platig, poses the problem whether our philosophy is more likely to be influenced by discoveries in the universe of space or in the tiny universe of the molecule. At every level in the scale from abstract philosophical questions to concrete technical ones comparable choices are posed. Resources are not infinitely enlargeable; hence, choices are unavoidable. In recent months, indeed since the papers in this volume were originally presented, there has been reason to believe that awareness of this need for choice has penetrated deeply in American society and, specifically, has influenced thought where decisions are made. For the first time, appropriations for NASA were significantly cut. There has been speculation that the Russians have also encountered the necessity to fix priorities in claims on resources.

One obvious consequence of the new mood may be a new willingness to re-examine the balance of advantage between competitive national space programs on the one hand and co-operative, perhaps more economical, ventures on the other hand. In this respect, it is encouraging to note that negotiations to internationalize the communications satellites system have been proceeding vigorously in recent months. The Soviet Union, moreover, has abandoned its stubborn opposition to space activities by private agencies and, as I write, exploration has begun of a possible relationship to the American-inspired system. The declaration unanimously adopted by the UN General Assembly on December 13, 1963, specifically referred to the possibility that "national activities in outer space" could be carried out "by nongovernmental entities." Thus, the door was opened to the paradoxical possibility of Soviet cooperation in an international satellite communications system inspired by the initiative of the Communications Satellite Corporation, a quasi-private American enterprise, whose stock has been sold in Wall Street, that citadel of American capitalism. In general, one can perhaps discern evolution in concepts of national interest, with respect at least to some aspects of space programs, in which the balance between competitive and cooperative emphases is in tension and may be shifting toward the latter.

This leads to the third observation. I have set forth the hypotheses that the interested governments are likely to pursue national interests and policies and national advantage in their space programs and that they will act competitively when national interests will thereby be served. I have also suggested that a rational view of national interests may lead to the conclusion that cooperation will sometimes prove more serviceable than competition. There is in this observation a principle of general relevance. To argue that governments pursue their national interests is not necessarily to conclude that they must therefore compete with other governments or display hostility to them. On the contrary, one does not even have to postulate an operative international standard of conduct, exerting autonomous pressures on interested governments, to conclude that governments may see persuasive reasons to acknowledge the interests of others in determining where their own interests lie. We do not have — to use a term employed by Professor Falk in this volume and elsewhere — a vertical international system in which states are subordinated to higher or more powerful authority. We remain in a horizontal system, in which it is not possible to discern a regimen to which governments must automatically accommodate. Even in such a system, however, a broad view of what constitutes the best exercise of autonomous national prerogatives is usually desirable and often necessary. The criterion of "reasonableness," which Professor Falk has set forth in another work, is a valid standard of wisdom and conscience in the judgments of individuals who have responsibility for the choice between cooperative and competitive options in national space programs.[2]

I have suggested that reasonableness — enlightened self-interest — may be at work in influencing the balance between cooperation and competition with respect to the non-military exploitation of space. Is there also some reason to believe that it may operate with respect to military uses of space? Obviously, the boundary between these two categories is an obscure one, as Professor Leon Lipson graphically observed: ". . . we do not know whether Gagarin's camera looked up, astronomically, or straight out, navigationally, or inward, clinically, or downward, curiously."[3] Leaving aside that obscurity, however, and dealing only with those activities which are predominantly military in their character, can one not again discern the same tension between competition and cooperation that has begun to appear with respect to non-military uses? Have there not been encouraging signs of convergence of interests between the Soviet Union and the United States on issues that had until recently divided them? Thus, enough mutuality of interest was carved out during extended explorations and negotiations concerning a nuclear test ban to permit agreement to ban nuclear explosions in space. Similarly, enough convergence occurred to permit the two leading powers to inspire the agreement of the General Assembly of the United Nations to the proposition that weapons of mass destruction should not be orbited in space. In both these instances, very pragmatic considerations were no doubt influential. Elements of cost and gain, narrowly viewed, were no doubt significant and led to or supported autonomous national conclusions that the inhibitions were in the national

---

[2] *Law, Morality and War in the Contemporary World,* Praeger, New York, 1963, p. 85.

[3] American Society of International Law, *Proceedings,* April 1961, p. 175.

interests of the space powers. Part of that calculation in each case was undoubtedly the awareness that a national decision to act competitively would with high probability generate a competitive response, the outcome of which was at best uncertainly advantageous and perhaps predictably disadvantageous. The fact that United States strategists could not convincingly argue that the United States would gain very much from being free to orbit a hydrogen bomb was an important factor in United States willingness to accept a prohibition against orbiting weapons of mass destruction. An important part of their calculations, no doubt, was the American interest in avoiding encouragement to the Soviet Union to seek a competitive advantage from a race to place bombs in space.

In another respect, too, convergence of interest appears to be occurring. The report [4] that Soviet space vehicles were conducting surveillance over United States terrain suggests that differences as to the legality of surveillance from space may be narrowing. Space observation might prove to be an important key to the open world of which statesmen orate.

In this limited history of converging interests, one may find some ground to hope that the fact that we live in a system which is predominantly "horizontal" does not mean that it may not become increasingly rational or that the balance between cooperation and competition may not progressively tilt in favor of the former.

Thus far in these brief remarks, I have dwelt, perhaps because of occupational bias, on the international rather than on the domestic implications of the subject of this volume. I recognize that international relations affecting space are but a segment of the subject "Space and Society." I have thus dealt with only some of the subjects which appear in the table of contents of this volume.

---

[4] *New York Times*, May 30, 1964, p. 1.

Nevertheless, there is a sense in which this choice of emphasis is broadly justified, apart from my own personal predilections in the matter. Experience seems to demonstrate that the international features of the problems have predominated and will predominate. This volume supports that judgment. In the words of Professor and Mrs. Taubenfeld, ". . . it is the insecurities, needs, and drives of the competing nations on earth which keep refueling their continual assault on space. . . ." We are aware of the fact that "space capacity is already part of the international balance of terror." We are also familiar with the propaganda and prestige benefits that pre-eminence in space has seemed to offer. I have already suggested that these competition-inspiring motivations may be tempered by growing awareness that national interest may not be served best by continuing to accept the risks and costs of the more competitive policy options. However, the relationship is a reciprocal one. It is clear that, so long as the incentive to compete internationally remains important, it will tend to dominate national choice in the allocation of scientific and economic resources among various space program alternatives and between space and other programs.

Clearly, these introductory remarks have done no more than to emphasize some of the questions we confront in entering upon the space age. All these questions are dealt with more detailed knowledge, in greater depth, and with greater penetration in the pages that follow. In contemplating what I have written here, as well as the contributions to this volume, one may well call to mind Edward Arlington Robinson's plaintive words:

Where was he going, this man against the sky?
You know not, nor do I.

JOSEPH E. JOHNSON, *President,*
Carnegie Endowment for International Peace.

Rita F. Taubenfeld

Howard J. Taubenfeld

MAN AND SPACE:
POTENTIALS, POLITICS, LEGAL CONTROLS

In the few years since October, 1957 when Sputnik I opened the space age in earnest, man's modest activities in outer space have demonstrated both the possible harvest of peaceful benefits and the potentials for international and national conflicts in interest which we may expect to reap. In considering the meaning of space developments in the context of politics, law and science, we must be clear that, though the technology and milieu are novel, we deal here as always with nations' relationship to nations, and man's relationship to man. We here attempt to set the stage for the papers which follow by indicating generally the political-legal conceptual and institutional background against which man's achievement in penetrating outer space can be viewed.

From the geocentric point of view, space can be taken at this time to include literally everything beyond a comparatively few miles above the earth's surface. There is as yet no political-legal definition of space. One important factor limiting our speculations is the scientist's current evaluation of man's ability to reach out into the infinite. With presently used or planned propulsion systems, it appears that man is limited to exploring the solar system for some generations, and perhaps forever. Thus we can avoid initially the problem of dealing with intelligent beings from other planetary systems, though the existence of life elsewhere is said to be a statistical certainty.

Man's penetration beyond the lower levels of the earth's atmosphere has come with startling rapidity. Since October, 1957, scores of satellites have been placed in orbit; space probes have developed sufficient thrust to break the grip of earth's gravity; the moon has been impacted and photographs have been made of its "dark" side. Military missiles which attain distances of 400 to 600 miles above the earth as they journey thousands of miles have been tested by the major powers, and other nations intend to join the club.

The satellites have already performed significant scientific tasks in the measurement of atmospheric density and the size and shape of the earth, and in studying the occurrence of micrometeorites, and ionization, temperatures, and radiations in space. Meteorological satellites have been launched and have functioned very well. The feasibility of earth-to-satellite and satellite-to-earth direct tele-communications has been established. Men (and a woman) have orbited the earth. Furthermore, as Doctor W. B. Klemperer has commented: "What looks like a great technological effort today, will be easy or even commonplace in ten or twenty or fifty years, if astronautical developments parallel those we have witnessed in aviation."

Man's ability to penetrate outer space has given rise both to speculations of new benefits to all mankind, to national and international controversy as to how space capabilities are to be utilized, and to increased fears for the security of all nations. The glowing possibilities include the promise of a vast increase in scientific knowledge about the nature of the universe and about the earth itself. There are expectation of great gains in many applied fields as well. The total scope and value of these gains in knowledge are by their nature still unpredictable but some fruits have already begun to ripen. Thus in addition to providing information about the basic nature of the weather and how it is "made," which itself might eventually be used to modify nature (not without substantial international political, economic and cultural effects on earth), a system of meteorological satellites can also provide reports on conditions over the vast areas of ocean, the polar regions and underdeveloped land masses, the ninety per cent of the globe from which little or no adequate information is currently available. It has been suggested that the more accurate forecasts thereby made more generally possible might be worth several billion dollars a year to the United States alone in farming, water resource conservation and prevention of loss of life and property. Navigation satellites could provide more accurate "fixes" for ships, submarines and aircraft under all weather conditions than is now possible. A system of communications satellites could provide instantaneous world-wide coverage at a cost independent of the distance involved, thus making a shrinking world dramatically smaller. Here again fascinating economic, cultural and political implications from space developments present themselves for speculation. Eventually, rapid transit between earth destinations may also be available for mail, cargo and passengers through use of rockets. If sufficiently low-cost service becomes feasible, a communications and transport revolution of more profound psychological, political and economic reverberations than the railway-steamship-telegraph revolution of the nineteenth century may be in the offing. The present nation-state system itself may be on the verge of technological and strategical obsolescence.

In addition to the close-in, earth-oriented potentials, there remain the unknown resources, strategic and material, of outer space with its possibly limitless potentials for the creation of new centers of human population and power. We have arrived at the brink of what may become a new and greater age of discovery.

Many possible uses of space offer material benefits to man, some perceivable even now, some shrouded by the very mysteries man is pursuing. We seek the unknown. What is the present value of the unknown? The ultimate cultural and political effects of man in space are even less foreseeable, yet the development of nuclear energy has shown us that these can be of overwhelming importance in any calculus of net gains and costs to mankind. If they seem to require us to live together more closely in peace, can we, considering our capacity to modify our present institutions? Do we really want to?

By contrast with these unknowns, the immediate economic costs of space pursuits, in terms of resources used or in terms of alternative investment opportunities foregone by national economies, though still complex, are relatively calculable. We know that even the more mundane space activities require vast inputs of capital for development, and most require cooperative efforts between national states for their maximum effectiveness and peaceful achievement. Thus they provide the nations and the international community with new challenges and new opportunities.

Considering all the genuine uncertainties involved, it is not surprising that expressions of ambivalence concerning the social utility and urgency of costly space programs have emanated from both space powers. The range of argument in the United States over a manned "moon shot" is itself indicative. What is the rational total allocation of national resources to space activities? Within this, what is the efficient suballocation between competing space uses and users? Which programs, civilian or military, should be pursued? Who should be allowed to reap the rewards of heavy national investment in space? It is reassuring to believe that society decides such issues as rationally as possible. We must also recognize the inherent limitations of rational calculation in the face of so many unknowns. To the usual formidable difficulties of "rational" social evaluation and efficient decision making in a democratic setting, which require a single set of decisions to accommodate the values and choices of millions of different individuals and, preferably, still to remain internally consistent, we add great uncertainties about the nature of the alternatives open for choice. Considerations of short run fiscal policy, military strategy, scientific curiosity and international prestige, as well as of past resource commitments and vested interests, will all affect the balancing of priorities and costs. Both for the United States, the Soviet Union and other nations, alone or in combination, the future sequence of activities and achievements in space will be a function of many variables and many guesses about the relevant uncertainties.

If the world were a single nation its decision processes would probably give heavy weighting to the relatively known factors, in this case to the costs in terms of resources which would otherwise be invested elsewhere. But in the present competitive multi-national world system it is the uncertainties which each state is under pressure to stress. The evaluations of competing powers are also interdependent; each has to give heavy weight to what it thinks the others will do. It is therefore almost impossible for a nation alone to decide with security not to pursue the unknown but knowable in space. The unknown has taken on a life of its own. Ultimately society's decisions on space questions must be arbitrary, though educated. The essays in this book cannot accurately and neatly balance all of the costs and gains of space ventures to society but they can shed light on some of the elements entering an educated social guess.

Since it is the insecurities, needs and drives of the competing nations on earth which keep refueling their continuing assault on space, the activities of states in this new theatre respond well to analysis by traditional tools. The classic if rarely clear-cut division between technical and political issues is useful for space problems too. As usual, only the former, those amenable to solution by technical cooperation, seem possible of relatively early and secure solution in the absence of more effective world institutions for the control of international conflict.

Technological cooperation can successfully precede such a millenium because it responds well to largely self-enforced international regulation. This occurs whenever it is clearly to the net advantage of the participating states not only to reach some generally accepted agreement but also to conform voluntarily to it. Failure to conform in such cases usually brings quick loss, often largely to the offending party. Rules of the road in the air and on the seas are thus very good examples of questions suitable for technical cooperation. They are obviously necessary and also do not detract from a state's power position and its ability to defend itself.

Unfortunately our second class of issues, those involving national security, power and prestige in a present or prospective sense and therefore the ability of national states to defend themselves (and to grow) is not amenable to such voluntary largely self-enforced programs of control. To ask a nation to cut its own power without real assurance that all other states will also do so proportionately would be to court disappointment. No national state could afford to conform honorably to such a request.

Within a developed nation, conflicts of interest over the relative and absolute distribution of old and new wealth and power are normally settled without violence by negotiation or by standardized administrative, legislative or legal techniques of compromise. Community institutions for peaceful conflict resolution, embodying the relevant group norms, including the need for order and therefore for compromise, are widely respected. Moreover the central government has overwhelming power, ranging from the capacity to mold opinion and thus to create a social value consensus to a virtual monopoly of enforcement organs, including the police and armed forces.

Regulation of similar issues internationally, even after an initial political bargain is negotiated between states on a power basis, requires the provision of adequate inspection and enforcement. These are necessary to reassure all honorable par-

ticipants that they will not be penalized for honest performance. They are more essential precisely because the sense of
shared identity and social responsibility and the institutions of
consensus creation, compromise, peaceful evaluation and
mutual assistance are so rudimentary in the international community, where each state must depend almost exclusively on
its own survival power. The preferences and incentives of
the competing nations and the overwhelming weight of
historical evidence indicate that the problem of keeping the
peace, on earth and in space, cannot be satisfactorily resolved
by self-policed, voluntary cooperation. This has not prevented
lawyers and statesmen as well, whether out of naivete, blind-
ness or pure political convenience, from picturing this group
of issues as amenable to "logical" jurisprudential analysis and
resolution, to assault by legal analogy, and to solution by the
development of voluntary, self-policed rules.

The limitation of the use of outer space to peaceful pursuits can be divided into two subsidiary problems: (1) keeping space from becoming another and even more terrifyingly
swift and brutal avenue of mass destruction on earth, as the
seas and the air have become, each in turn, as war technology
developed, and (2) keeping outer space from becoming still
another theatre for great power rivalries in peacetime and
hence another source of hatred, fear, competitive power disadvantage, conflict and war. This is the dual problem of
peace in space. Neither is amenable to easy solution through
avowals of national self-denial. Unless firmly forestalled,
national "security" considerations will inevitably, of necessity,
be stretched to include control of celestial resources when and
if they become valuable and attainable. More immediately,
space has already proven its military potential in such fields
as observation, communications and communications interference and as a possible testing ground, storehouse and highway
for nuclear destruction.

Most space activities have an inherent dual capacity.
Thus, satellites equipped to perform "peaceful" observations

necessary for mapping, meteorological and similiar surveys will furnish information inevitably useful for military purposes when they report what they "see" to the national state which launched them. Moreover, without inspection at the launching site or a capture in space when that becomes feasible, it is not even possible to be completely certain that a space vehicle is in fact destined for a stated peaceful purpose, perhaps in accordance with some international technical agreement, rather than on some immediate or eventual warlike mission. Without direct inspection, present techniques are simply inadequate for differentiating on the ground or during the powered phase between rockets used to launch peaceful satellites and intercontinental missiles. Indeed, radar warning systems, themselves an important balancing item in the present world system, are probably destined to become less satisfactory, regardless of the launcher's intentions, due to the existence of substantial numbers of objects orbiting the earth. Space capacity can also facilitate the intentional jamming of warning systems; it has already been shown, for example, that a high altitude nuclear blast over the Indian Ocean might black out areas in Western Russia. Erroneous attack reports occurred even before the intercontinental missile became a reality. In a world of weapons which move increasingly rapidly and are increasingly deadly, so that literally only a few minutes may be available between detection and the possibility of partial survival and of retaliation, governments may not be able to afford the luxury of soul searching or authentication before reaction. Short of an actual inspection of payloads before launching or, alternatively, of a program of launchings solely under the direction and control of an international organization, the nerve-wracking military implications of almost any human penetration of outer space will remain inescapable.

Peaceful technical cooperation in space activities would offer no assistance either in the elimination of the possibility of military clashes in space itself which may arise in apparently still far off "colonial" type struggles or in other already important security dimensions of space activities when the capacity to intercept space vehicles is developed. However remote from earth initially, such clashes might, like those of the past on the high seas, spread and precipitate military action on earth. In short, in the decentralized international system which lacks both the capacity to separate neatly the peaceful uses of space for control by international technical agencies, and the institutions needed to guarantee peaceful conflict resolution and national security in general, "there is no good reason to suppose that man's normal potential for good or evil would in any way be altered by his advance into space or that national struggles for supremacy would not simply be projected onto the larger screen of the cosmos unless checked at the very outset" by an intelligent, comprehensive, equitable program of international controls. It is easy to see this. It is not easy to suggest the best approach to such a program.

The crux of the difficulty is that space capacity is already part of the international balance of terror. Space disarmament is but one segment of the broader, overshadowing problem of world peace and disarmament with which the world has wrestled with growing need but without sustained success.

It is easy to feel that the problem of assuring peaceful cooperative progress in space is a Gordian knot, inextricably intertwined with highly sensitive military security issues. Apparently, it will be necessary to achieve a general settlement and disarmament with substitute world institutions for law and order on earth. Failing that, the most fruitful alternative would appear to be to separate out and remove from earth's antagonistic, competitive national states all of the potentially military space activities—which means all space activities. For such a policy of sector disarmament and internationalization to have the faintest chance of success politically, there would have to be a willingness to share the fruits of exploiting new frontiers internationally, a willingness which has been universally lacking in the past. The suggested program would also have to provide national states with the positive assurance that an agreement for peaceful, cooperative, supranational exploitation and use of space will not prove detrimental to national security. Thus, a satisfactory international organization and control of space penetration on a sector approach probably requires that the pre-internationalization balance of power be reestablished, and then that the banishment of national operations be made effective. In short, it implies that an effective international inspection system is necessary and that an effective international enforcement system for space is probably necessary as well. Our sovereign states have thus far been unable to accommodate themselves to such drastic political innovations. Indeed any effective broad program of disarmament on earth or in space clearly implies the creation of a more powerful central international organization than self-interested states have ever been willing to tolerate. Effective sector disarmament and internationalization of space is not inconceivable; indeed, if possible anywhere, perhaps outer space is the most suitable starting place. It is nevertheless such a radical departure from past experience with national preferences as to appear politically unlikely. Less satisfactory, more modest first approaches to the neutralization and internationalization of space deserve analysis; rational decision making nevertheless requires that their defects not be glossed over.

On a more hopeful note, a converse may be true. Science is constantly making detection and inspection easier. Space instrumentalities may soon provide an alternative system to an international presence within disarming nations. They will some day be capable of providing reliable international inspection for detection of rocket launchings, nuclear explosions, massing of troops and the like and hence may serve as part of a system for safeguarding peace. This is perhaps the major way in which space use will make the world smaller. Less will have to remain unknown. It seems useless in this case as well to request national self-denial or to try to ignore or reverse technological advance. Information that can be obtained will be obtained, either to buttress the peace or to win the conflict. The challenging question is how it could most creatively be used to strengthen peace. The soundest approach may well be the establishment of exclusive, shared international systems of information gathering. To design now an international regime which would not capitulate to one or the other of the two space powers and which would pursue vigorously a program involving an international right to knowledge to buttress the peace is, to say the least, a challenging problem. Does *any* nation really want to share strategic information?

The basic causes for man's age old failure to unite to maintain peace do not disappear at the nonexistent boundary between air space and outer space. These causes are only partly systemic. To be sure, the system is inherently so sensitive to changes in and threats to national security that it is self-reinforcing; national self-preservation absolutely requires strength, not saintliness, honesty or self-denial. But man is not inevitably trapped in the national state system. He is there partly by preference and historical choice.

The explanations are complex but ultimately man in society thinks primarily in terms of the interests of those with whom he can and has been trained to identify personally. It is to his personal psychological and apparent or real economic self-interest to do so. Indeed nationalism is self-interest writ large. Sweeping considerations of that broader focus of identity, the human race—self-interest writ larger—even when sincere or even necessary in the nuclear-space age are not consistent with his training and ingrained preferences. They conflict with genuine, if socially created, cultural compartmentalization and with the inherited and man-made differences in wealth, power and opportunity which in turn have been the product of divergent cultural emphases as well as of geography, history and luck. Add to this that the unstable system itself inhibits international experimentation of all kinds since the price of failure may be extinction for the nation and its ethos and culture, and great personal loss for the contemporary individual who is the creature and creation of that culture. In a world in which men have repeatedly sacrificed personal for national survival, we now face problems requiring an overriding world ethos and identity as foundations for worldwide institutions of order with equity. Viable solutions cannot be personally or nationally pleasant or easy.

History and logic may discourage optimism but, since we are here to discuss our discouragement, they clearly do not yet justify despair. Indeed logical systems, though unavoidable, are themselves dangerous in the social sciences; out of necessity, they consciously oversimplify the relevant facts and then embalm the structural relationships distilled out of the past. The resultant predictions tend to be more apocalyptic than even so unadaptable a thing as man's social behavior justifies. The international community has neither solved its earthly political problems nor converted space into an elysian field, free of such earthly blight. Ignoring all summons to logic, the world has moved slowly and in a rather stately way into space. Eschewing all overall "grand" designs, the general approach of the major powers has been pragmatic and piecemeal. The accomplishments have been noteworthy. Are they sufficient?

First of all, a considerable amount of international cooperation in scientific and technical programs has been developed over the years both in the "nongovernmental" scientific community and in officially organized intergovernmental arrangements. Indeed, the space age was ushered in under the programs of the International Geophysical Year (IGY), the experiment in international scientific cooperation in many fields which ran from mid-1957 through 1958. That program was promoted by the nominally nongovernmental International Council of Scientific Unions and was participated in by scientists from some sixty-six nations with active governmental backing, financing and support. It was essentially a program involving coordination of nationally proposed and executed programs. Outer space was one of the areas of special interest within the program. While many examples of cooperative efforts in space activities exist, there were limitations from the outset as to the extent of cooperation achieved. No full agreement was ever reached on the amount or type of information to be supplied by launchers to the world data centers, a significant gap in a supposedly international research program. It appears that the Russians always regarded the launchings as an integral part of their domestic military program and were therefore simply unwilling to give away the primary data which might reveal military rocket capabilities or the codes used for telemetering information from the satellites.

Despite this not altogether unblighted record of scientific cooperation, negotiations were begun during the IGY in an effort to assure continued cooperation in outer space, leading to the formation of the Committee on Space Research (COSPAR). However, by 1958 the intimate relationship between scientific, military and prestige ends in space was quite clear and COSPAR's subsequent history has been marred by unmistakably political disputes, for example, a Soviet scientific "walkout" over "parity" which ended only in January, 1960. International cooperative scientific programs remain under this cloud despite the fact that by 1963, as we shall see, space activities were touched by the more general Soviet-U.S. political thaw, reflecting their increasing common political interest in the maintenance of the present international *status quo* on earth. Thus, early in 1963, they were able to agree on limited cooperation outside COSPAR in a meteorological satellite program, joint communications experiments using a passive reflector satellite and contributions of data to the World Magnetic Survey.

The United States also has cooperative programs for launching space vehicles, tracking, meteorological studies and the like with many non-Communist countries. All these nationally controlled programs for sharing are also inherently subject to the moods of foreign policy and do not realistically provide a secure substitute for a nation's own program of research in the new technology for those states which might hope to compete with the two present space powers. This is perhaps the most significant long run technological-political fact of the space age. Few medium size economies have felt they could afford to enter the space competition alone and none has as yet produced dramatic successes. As a result, other joint ventures on a regional scale such as the European programs for space research and launch vehicle development, ESRO and ELDO, have been launched as well.

The minimum efficient size national economic base required for large-scale space technology may change after the initial period of huge capital investment in probing and exploration; or space and its technology may turn out to be unimportant economically and politically. At present the middle states can probably afford to mark time. If space or space technology should prove dramatically important economically, militarily or politically, and national space capacity or its use remain very costly in resources, the only alternatives to effective regional development with arrangements for sharing of control for such nations may well be the secure, shared international development of space, or continued reliance, without shared controls, on a major space power.

Can they afford to trust their protectors in nuclear or space programs either to protect them as *they* would like or to give them their idea of a "fair" share of whatever the gains from the new technology turn out to be? In sum, where knowledge is, or could be power, the pursuit of knowledge is clearly a political activity. As a result, national investment in space science has turned out to be more sensitive and scientific cooperation has been less secure than other more mundane, more pressing, less mysterious forms of technical cooperation in space.

Thus, the problems of allocating scarce, economically valuable radio channels for space vehicles, space communications systems and radio astronomy has already been acted on by an international organization, the International Tele-communications Union. Similar type problems exist in such areas as the allocation of liability for damage caused on earth by a space vehicle's falling, the creation of techniques for identifying the nationality of a space vehicle, the establishment of rules or understandings for the return of vehicles and personnel which fall or land in other than the launching country and contamination of space and of earth on return from space. On such issues there is now not only a substantial consensus among Soviet and American spokesmen but the General Assembly, in the fall of 1963, adopted an agreed statement of principles on state responsibility and liability for space activities, ownership and the right of return of space vehicles and international consultation in advance of certain types of space activities. More specific agreements in such fields are also anticipated. Other technical and therefore potentially soluble problems will become more pressing only when space traffic increases. These include the provision of space navigation and similar codes, provision for standards and certificates of qualification for space personnel, and, eventually, rules governing the carriage of passengers and goods, legal transactions in space, and relations with and between humans on the celestial bodies.

In addition to the I. T. U. and the UN itself, there are several existent intergovernmental technical agencies in these and clearly analogous fields already dealing with similar problems closer to earth. There are the many agencies dealing with navigation facilities and the coordinating work of the World Meteorological Organization. Even now, the International Civil Aviation Organization (ICAO) and the International Maritime Consultative Organization (IMCO) are charged with setting safety standards, personnel qualifications, rules for safe transit and the like in their respective spheres.

Two concluding caveats about technical cooperation in space activities are indicated by experience. First, where valuable assets are involved, as is already the case with communications satellites, functional cooperation has a severe limitation; it does not necessarily assure a "fair" division of the enterprise, the control of the new activity or the costs and profits derived from it. The intentions and bargaining positions of the powers remain the most important determinants of the international distribution of the gains from man's activity in space, as elsewhere, which may be unfortunate for all those without power. Distribution in space as elsewhere is a "political problem"; after the political solution, the distributive choice may, of course, be effectuated by international technical cooperation.

Second, successful programs of technical cooperation in space activities seem, if anything, even more limited to times of general peace than such programs in less inherently strategic arenas and activities. During major war, and perhaps during times of major crisis as well, we must expect that whatever space systems and uses prove convenient will be used, whatever the sober peacetime commitments undertaken concerning orderly cooperation in such fields as communications, navigation and meteorology.

To gain some perspective on the implications of what has been achieved so far by voluntary, self-policed cooperation in our second broad class of issues, the frankly strategic, security-suffused cases, it is instructive to review the brief history of the international pursuit of peace in space. Except for observation satellites, there is thus far less conflict between the political positions of the two space powers than might have been anticipated. Initially both the United States and the Soviet Union approached space politics cautiously, with policies reminiscent of those maintained for the Antarctic. Neither made a claim; both reserved the freedom to do so and attempted to establish the basis for such action if it should ever prove politic. A Soviet rocket placed the Soviet coat of arms on the moon while Russia disclaimed covetous intentions. At the same time, both Soviet and American spokesmen and writers urged that space be reserved for peaceful activities. The concept of national sovereignty in outer space was criticized by all, the Soviet writer Korovine labeling it "unscientific geocentrism, a return from Copernicus to Ptolemy," for example.

It is essential to recall nevertheless that *all* nations do claim, and defend with arms, their airspace. Neither space power has to date committed itself as to where this zone of sovereignty ends and outer space begins. Some American spokesmen have, in the past, suggested that airspace be defined elastically, if at all, and that, in general, no line should be drawn limiting a sovereign claim until "we have a great deal more knowledge." Both space powers agree that the principles of the UN Charter, including the right of self-defense under Article 51, are applicable to space activities. Each obviously claims the legal right to defend itself anywhere in space. Perhaps most significant of all is the fact that both nations have brought pragmatism to space activities, to the political as well as the technical and legal issues. Neither has desired a comprehensive space solution or a grand design involving international controls for law and order in space. Ultimately, neither has been willing to be limited in its "peaceful" pursuit of whatever it turns out space offers, especially since this may prove to be primarily military advantage.

Both space powers have been, at different times, instrumental in bringing problems connected with the use of space to the UN. This forum has been useful for their purposes and has played an undeniably creative role in facilitating the achievement of political agreements acceptable to both. The history of space power maneuvering in UN space negotiations is itself instructive.

In the course of the disarmament talks of 1957, before any satellites were in orbit, the United States called the world's attention to the dangers inherent in the development of outer space weapons and offered to enter into any "reliable agreement" to "mutually control the outer space missile and satellite development." This led to a General Assembly resolution in November, 1957, providing, among many other things, for a technical committee "to study the design of an inspection system. . . . To assure that the sending of objects through outer space will be exclusively for peaceful and scientific purposes."

In January, 1958, Secretary Dulles proposed the formation of an international commission to insure the use of outer space for peaceful purposes only. In March, the Soviet Union proposed that the next session of the General Assembly consider "Banning the use of cosmic space for military purposes, the elimination of foreign bases on the territories of other countries, and international cooperation in the study of cosmic space," through a UN agency. In September, the United States temporized by proposing that the Assembly consider the question of a program for cooperation in outer space activities. An *ad hoc* study committee to report on this subject was created. The Soviet dropped its suggestion of a UN agency.

Even this modest entrance of the United Nations onto the space scene was incapable of enlisting the support of both space powers, as the Soviet Union pursued its policy of insistence on parity in all arrangements, and on this the Western powers would not then yield. Meeting in early 1959 without the participation of the Soviet bloc, the United Arab Republic or India, the Committee prepared a report carefully avoiding action beyond the identification of problem areas in which the United Nations and other international organizations could be helpful.

In the fall of 1959, a new, permanent study group was constituted, the UN Committee on the Peaceful Uses of Outer Space. The Soviet space "veto" was of necessity informally accepted and "soft parity" was accorded the Soviet bloc. Despite Western power urging and despite parity, Russia, in a relatively strong technological position, still temporized.

There were no meetings of this new Committee in 1960, and only a single brief one in 1961.

In the fall of 1961 however, the United States adopted a more aggressive approach. In a strong speech, President Kennedy carried the issue of space cooperation to the General Assembly in September. If on analysis his suggestions were modest, they appealed to the increasingly concerned small powers, anxious for at least some declaratory action on space. So much support was obtained that, in December, Resolution 1721 was unanimously adopted. Specifically, that Resolution commends to all states for their guidance the principles that:

International law, including the Charter of the United Nations, applies to outer space and celestial bodies; and that:

Outer space and celestial bodies are free for exploration and use by all States in conformity with international law and are not subject to national appropriation.

If these principles are accepted as law—and the United States maintains that they *are* already law—the major powers have to some extent limited their freedom of action, though the nature of the non-national regime for outer space, the moon and the planets remains to be specified. Why have both accepted (and even urged) this approach?

No doubt the transition from stalemate to unanimous support for this UN resolution on space reflects both the pressures of widespread popular support for some sign of progress and the real interests of the two space powers most affected. Nothing was changed respecting the peacetime military uses of close-in space. By 1961 it had become apparent that the assault on deep space and the celestial bodies would be protracted and costly and that, even more than in the Antarctic, effective exclusive occupation and use of the celestial bodies would be difficult to establish. Antarctic politics suggest that there is obvious utility in precluding claims to exclusive sovereignty which have to be disregarded in fact as ineffective or absurd but which remain a political nuisance.

Furthermore self-denying rules limiting national claims will always be least effective in restraining the strongest powers, which retain greater capacity to change their positions, if they should decide that their overwhelming needs call for exclusive control of some area in space or some celestial body. Should space accessibility change dramatically, new forms of exclusive control without claims to sovereignty can doubtless be invented by those with the greatest technological capacity to assert them. Moreover the space powers can always use their historical lead to make official claims if necessary. No effective obstacle in the form of a precluding alternative, international regime has been formally proposed, much less accepted.

The 1961 Resolution had a further provision worthy of special note. It called for an international registry at the UN of all objects launched into space. This is not a prior warning, much less an on-site inspection which would be necessary for determining the true nature of satellite missions and contents. It is interesting to report the compliance achieved: The United States, after initial reluctance to report *all* launchings rather than only successful orbital launches, now complies fully with this recommendation but has adopted security techniques in the reporting of military vehicles launches. The Soviet Union has apparently reported most, but not all, of its launchings.

The UN's revamped Outer Space Committee met in 1962 and early 1963 with some progress in its Technical Subcommittee but none in its Legal Subcommittee, which dealt with what are politically sensitive issues. By mid-1963, Russia again proved ready, against a backdrop of the continuing, intensifying Russian-Chinese rift, to conclude several dramatic, not too costly, political arrangements with the United States, some involving space activities.

Most widely discussed of all is the partial Nuclear Test Ban Treaty which barred explosions and testing in outer space as well as in the atmosphere. In addition, Russia was now amenable to a UN resolution banning the placing in orbit of weapons of mass destruction. Next, a resolution adopted in December filled in some features of the open régime for space by declaring that states should assume full responsibility for activities in space by themselves and their nationals, that due consultations be held before potentially harmful activities are undertaken in space and that space vehicles and space voyagers be safely returned to their national state in the event of disaster.

This is where we stand to date. Some progress has been made in the control of nations in space on a piecemeal basis. The list is impressive but so are the gaps. It would be misleading to overlook the omissions in these three major self-restraining political agreements, the ban on orbiting weapons, the test ban in space and the "open" régime.

The major deficiency is implicit in the fact that there is no provision for international inspection or enforcement in any of them. While the United States feels secure in its own ability to monitor space for nuclear radiation, any evidence of testing so gained remains national, or at best multinational, not "impartial." Though the United States can now monitor launchings with some confidence and can deduce partial information on space vehicles and their contents from orbital and other characteristics, the ban on orbiting weapons is in fact presently inadequately inspected and may remain inadequately inspectable for some time. The uninspiring performance in mere registering of space launches suggests that neither power would welcome an on-site inspection prior to launching. Unless the world community were greatly changed, any claimed right to unilateral inspection in peacetime by means of national interception of satellites in space, when that becomes feasible, would lead to as bitter political disputes in space as it has on the seas. In sum, at present and for some time to come we cannot in fact *know* what the space powers are placing in space.

In a world of self-defending sovereigns, we can, with some risks, postpone the answer to Fred Charles Iklé's question: "After Detection—What?", but, if we are serious, we can never postpone adequate inspection, national if not international. All we can expect from inadequately inspected, nationally policed programs of self-denial in strategic matters is that, if the nations were not planning on doing the prohibited act anyway, and if they do not find it in their national interest to do it in the future, the ban on orbital weapons represents a relatively costless international exercise. If an effective agreement were really necessary, such a relatively uninspected one could prove dangerous to the peace. As representatives of the nation more likely to honor uninspected agreements unilaterally, American negotiators presumably considered such destabilizing dangers unimportant in this case. The U. S. second strike deterrent on earth is considered presently immune to destruction.

In what way have the two space powers effectively limited themselves by sponsoring this General Assembly declaration? They have publicly recommended to the world the desirability of prohibiting the orbiting of weapons which, for safety, cost and other reasons, neither apparently wanted to develop at present. The existence of such a public declaration may itself help to induce conformity, even on the part of the Soviet Union, even in times when it may become less convenient. But so long as performance remains incapable of corroboration or refutation, the only demonstrable achievement is the sacrifice of some freedom to exchange threats based on orbiting weapons of mass destruction. Conformity with this verbal restraint is directly observable by all.

The ban is valuable at present principally for its net psychological effect. It can always be argued that *any* agreement between the Big Powers may increase good will and decrease tensions between them. Obviously both powers retain formidable capacity to challenge and exacerbate one another. The crucial issue is whether the agreement will in fact be used as a substitute for, rather than a precursor of, more meaningful and effective agreements. If so, its major effect will have been to help the Great Powers delude each other and other nations into believing that impressive steps in neutralizing space had been taken while in fact they have largely marked time. The net psychological effect of the weapons ban can only be revealed by the future performance of the Powers in subsequent negotiations. Judged as a pure statement of principle, *if* it is not destabilizing and *if* it is not in fact used as a substitute for politically feasible, more substantial agreement, then it is at worst no less creative and no more costly than any other broad declaratory international statement, such as, for example, the Kellogg-Briand Pact of 1928 which "outlawed" war for the parties.

The Nuclear Test Ban Treaty is clearly an inflexible *"status quo"* agreement: it installs a nationally inspected continuation of the bilateral nuclear monopoly. We here need only to evaluate this complex agreement sufficiently to indicate its potentials and implications for space testing.

The widespread popularity of the Treaty indicates that those nations which do not aspire to nuclear and space power in the near future are even more afraid of other states which may so aspire, and of the simple risk of numbers, than of the present situation in which two giants share the power of life and death for all, including themselves. What of the prospective fellow giants? They are not bound by the treaty, nor are they necessarily irrational in trusting themselves as much as Russia and the United States. Is it likely that, after French and Chinese proven capacities increase the number of nuclear giants, all states now bound will feel they can afford to remain so? The answer will vary no doubt with the nature of the social and governmental structure within the non-nuclear, dependent states and with the state of the relationships between the two major nuclear powers and their client states. Presumably the greater the real national strategic independence of the clients, the more important would be the techniques of assuring reciprocal respect and confidence between the members and genuinely integrated control of military and strategic policy within the bloc.

In addition, one can guess that authoritarian governments and states with aggressive new or different ideologies, races or cultures which, in the long run, are least assimilable into any existent power group, would be least likely to be satisfied permanently with a perpetual *status quo* structure of world power. The Arab or African states, for example, are likely, when they are ready, to feel justified in seeking a domestic nuclear capacity through testing if necessary despite their commitment to the Test Ban. If they test, what about those who in turn will feel threatened by them?

If we assume that the Treaty's intent was not primarily to embalm the present *status quo* and to prevent the spread of nuclear power to more nations or the "less responsible" nations, but was to reduce the risks of atmospheric contamination, then a ban on tests in outer space makes less sense. It has been suggested that deep space might provide the safest testing area, avoiding the fallout problem entirely. The need for testing itself could also be reduced by some system of sharing of nuclear information or weapons, at least with those states which would and could test and learn for themselves in any event. Indeed this would convert the Treaty from an inflexible to a flexible *status quo* agreement, a more viable type of instrument of social control. This unlikely and perhaps risky alternative runs counter to the general hostility to nuclear sharing among the nations, which itself suggests that the *status quo* political aspects of the Treaty have been in fact more important than the pollution control aspects, even to the majority non-nuclear powers.

The hope remains that the existence of a treaty makes it more difficult even for the Soviet Union to decide upon an open breach. If so, the Big Two may have freed themselves from unnecessary competition in testing and have provided at least some reduction in potential fallout pollution. Nevertheless, it is only a few years since the voluntary test moratorium was ignored by the Soviet Union despite inevitable worldwide disapproval. Significantly this disapproval was soon deflected to the innocent party, the United States, which felt impelled to test as well in self-defense to maintain the technological balance. The Soviet action, it must be recalled, required months of secret, undetected preparation in advance of the announcement prior to the overt acts. Thus the conforming parties shared the onus and enjoyed a strategic disadvantage as well.

While reliance on a national inspection system has these drawbacks, reliance on a national enforcement system has all the traditional dangers. Since international enforcement is not provided for, it is always possible that one or both of the present nuclear giants will try to impose a continuation of the present bilateral nuclear monopoly. The overwhelming acceptance of the Treaty which enshrines the *status quo* might well be used as justification for actual or threatened unilateral intervention or retaliation against nuclear hopefuls, a doubtful way to keep the peace. In sum, it is difficult not to feel nervous about the ability of any inflexible, self-denying *status quo* agreement between sovereigns once the actual distribution of power potentials begins to change. When that occurs, if underground testing, though still permitted, proves inadequate, it might be clearly preferable to facilitate rather than to ban tests in deep space.

By far the most significant of these arrangements in space politics was the earliest, the self-denying declaration that outer space and the celestial bodies are free for use by all and are not subject to national appropriation. This too is a type of *status quo* oriented agreement; it favors the strong. It exemplifies nevertheless a different, more flexible and viable concept of the *status quo* than does the Test Ban Treaty. As power relationships change, the new structure is automatically accommodated within the standing rules. Ultimately, most Western societies rely on a moving *status quo* system for the "impersonal," efficient distribution of opportunity, wealth and power. The classical economist's ideal market system, which remains the most relevant abstract model of Western-type, decentralized, individualistic community organization, implies just such a structure of decentralized group distribution making. Since, in practice, human institutions are imperfect in many ways, the aggregate results of all the individual acts of self-interest in society usually diverge from the requisites of the general interest and the community's more important ethical values. In most actual decentralized societies, the main business of collective decision making by the constitutional organs of government, after group survival itself, is the provision of agreed corrections for the effects of these inevitable systemic imperfections. In the international system where there is no effective central authority, who corrects the actions of the states? Who speaks for man?

As we have noted, neither space power has wished to submit to a comprehensive regime of internationally controlled order even if limited to space activities and even if it would be designed to allow the maximum pursuit of national self interest consistent with effective international controlled conflict resolution. Thus the analogy of the free seas has been stressed as a prototype for the international regime for space, as if the islands and continents in the "free seas" were never subjected to national appropriation and as if the high seas themselves had not seen much battle and blood.

Surely even under an effective international agreement following the pattern of General Assembly Resolution 1721 of 1961, when man develops the necessary capabilities, questions of occupation, use and shares in the exploitation of space resources by humans, in government service and without, will arise. This will all require some regime which provides peaceful decision making and conflict resolution as well as mere functional cooperation. The variety of presumably even more remote problems which earth administration of substantial planetary colonization might create is staggering but obvious.

Many of the problems raised here are not upon us now. How important they will become remains a mystery like so much else concerning space. The predilection for a free hand and for a pragmatic problem-by-problem approach is consistent with American philosophical and legal traditions and with the space powers' foreseeable short run self interest. It may not prove intelligent for the long run. If we use history at all, it should be in just such cases where longer run "scientific" prediction eludes the social scientist and the issues are important. Like the physician, we must use our "wisdom", the fruits of our experience, as well as our incomplete science. Any self-policed, self denying rule by states to limit their space activities to "peaceful" pursuits and analogous commitments to permit free access or to keep celestial possessions or spheres of influence demilitarized must raise anew the ghosts of earlier experiments with colonial free access and with "neutralized" and "demilitarized" areas. Even allowing for the great psychological and social changes of the climate in which the national state system persists into the nuclear-space age, history suggests that an open regime at best implies a free-for-all competition between nations, a dangerous way to play a dangerous game.

There are of course valid objections to overdirection of man's assault on the unknown. Experience indicates that it is practical and indeed probably necessary that many of the specific legal problems of space be solved as they arise. This can be accomplished most effectively within an intelligently organized international space regime. Thus, the common law, that most gradual and pragmatic of legal systems, developed within a reasonably adequate governmental framework, something that international law in general and "space" in particular now lack. Law needs a creator. The legal system will follow and reflect the general political settlement for space, or the lack of a settlement. Without a general settlement, technical and legal problems will in general be solved only when they are unavoidable and in the usual manner, with each state acting as its own domestic and international politics dictate at the moment of international decision. They will remain settled only as long as the settlement suits the major powers' national interest, as they see it. Political problems, those of sharing and of peace and security in space, will be resolved as always by contests of power which, in the current jungle world, always include, as the ultimate court of appeal, both limited and general war.

This does not mean the General Assembly's declarations of principles are without value. Even the negative rule against exclusionary sovereign claims is useful in itself as a moral position and also because it can facilitate a retrenchment in exhaustively expensive "crash" space programs. Again, without a substitute regime, neither power can really rely on the self-policed self denial of the other in space and both remain under pressure to continue to pursue the unknown, despite the expense.

If we are lucky and this expensive space investment turns out to be relatively fruitless except for inherently sharable, peaceful resources such as scientific knowledge, the choice of regime will remain unimportant. Of course, the interdependent competition between the space powers will continue to induce overinvestment in space relative to its promise and that of other more worthy investments from a world point of view. If we are unlucky and space mastery yields great strategic value for the great investment of resources, the choice of having no functioning overall international regime may prove disastrous and irreversible. Even in well regulated communities, achieving peaceful agreement on the appropriate distribution of great good fortune is bitterly disputed. In the unintegrated international system, where there is little spirit of community or sharing, and where any new source of wealth and power affects the balance of power and the relative survival prospects of the members, a rich find, once available, would not lightly be surrendered to a regime of world control and sharing, even one which was designed to protect the legitimate vested interests of the initial investors.

Thus far, space activities have proved neither fruitless nor fantastically rich in yield, except perhaps to science. Such experience as we have acquired with voluntary sharing of information and of potentially profitable investment opportunity is not entirely encouraging. If the stakes mount no more rapidly than in the past and the celestial bodies remain virtually economically unattainable, the spread from earth into space of a decentralized, permissively competitive, open regime may be good enough or flexible or inchoate enough to change with perceived needs. But why risk it?

Surely the scientists' repeated wish to conduct research in space unfettered politically is disingenuous, if not dishonest considering the huge investment of resources required for their experiments. In any case the preferences of a small pressure group do not move whole societies to take such risks. Indeed both space powers do fetter their scientific and academic communities, to the point of largely choosing the projects which are to receive social support. We must assume that the space powers are not yet ready to agree to organized world-wide sharing of the fruits of their competitive assault on space, that they mean to gain competitive advantage therefrom.

Are we to be left to hope for great waste so that the gains from space will prove small and not destabilizing? Is it possible that the nations will somehow become more socially responsible, despite the atavistic system, and more able to agree freely to controlled freedom, in President Eisenhower's words: "this time—and in time."?

The technological problems are being assaulted on many fronts; some of the legal and political problems—those less intertwined with direct security considerations—are similarly coming under national and international control. Problems in the fields of the economic and social implications of the space age are, however, just beginning to come into view.

Technologically we are already in outer space; the balance of the implications for mankind, for good or for ill, is still unclear. The wisest national and international approaches to new or heightened problems are certainly open to study, debate, and even crusade. It is to some of these problems, including those of a world threatened by space developments, that the following papers are devoted.

2

Robert Jastrow

SCIENCE, THE SCIENTIST AND SPACE DEVELOPMENTS

I should like to make some comments concerning the context in which the scientific objectives of the space program should be considered and some of the positive and negative aspects which can be foreseen in its future development.

The program is a large one, with over 5 billion dollars requested for the fiscal 1964 - 65, and it appears to be having substantial effects, both direct and indirect, on many aspects of our national life. The NASA laboratories and operational activities involve a government force of 30,000 employees. 840 industrial contractors support NASA in the execution of its projects. Their work involves a force of 500,000 in private industry. Approximately 120 universities support NASA in research and in the training of space scientists and engineers. It is too early to make a full assessment of the impact of these activities, but even at this early stage we already can identify some elements in the basic structure of this new enterprise.

First, it is a program of research and exploration which produces scientifically valuable results, practical applications, and indirect technological benefits.

Second, it is fundamentally an international program. Its research objectives and practical applications are concerned with the properties of the earth as an entire planet, and they involve scientific projects which cut across national boundaries. The man-in-space program, scientific satellites, and space probes all require international networks of tracking stations and extensive supporting operations.

Moreover, other countries see the benefits of space research to their science and technology and are attempting to develop their own programs in this field. In order to assist these nations, totaling approximately 55, NASA and other government agencies have constructed an extensive machinery for the international exchange of ideas and talents. NASA itself is committed to a number of international programs: graduate fellowships, research appointments for senior scientists, cooperative association in the meteorological communications satellite programs, and technical assistance in space programs of other countries.

Third, the space program benefits our society in the most general sense through the exploration of new territories and the ability to make a new attack on old problems.

My own concern with the program is confined to its very specific applications to scientific investigations. These are only a small part of the cost of the program, but they are extremely important, because out of them comes the understanding of the laws which govern our physical environment — the understanding which determines the circumstances of our lives today and which will condition our achievements in the future.

The history of science demonstrates that we need not expect a long wait before the results of space research play a role in our lives. The interval between basic discoveries and their applications to practical affairs has decreased steadily during the course of the scientific revolution. The lag was 37 years from Maxwell's publication of the laws of the electromagnetic field in 1864 to the first radio experiments by Marconi; 10 years from the discovery of the neutron in 1932 to the first nuclear reactor, and 6 years from the invention of the transistor in 1948 to the first transistorized amplifier on the market. Based on this record, some of the important discoveries and advances of space science should feed back into our lives within the decade.

I should like to give some examples of basic and applied investigations in science, which, while being overwhelmingly important, also have a special interest because they cannot in any way be conducted from the ground.

As a first example: In the realm of pure science, we consider the complex of questions relating to the structure of the universe in the large — the cosmic abundances of the elements, the evolution of stars and galaxies, the formation of the sun and planets — how we came to be here in the physical sense. All the information we have about the world around us on a large scale — the composition of the stars, their life histories from the time of birth in a chance condensation out of the gas and dust of interstellar space, to the eventual destruction in the explosion of the supernova — comes to us in the form of light radiated from the surfaces of these stars, which penetrates through the atmosphere to reach the surface of the earth where it is collected by telescopes and analyzed spectroscopically.

Most of this starlight is absorbed in the atmosphere of the earth, and only a pitifully small fraction of all the radiation actually reaches telescopes on the surface, that is, namely, the thin shaft of light in the visible region plus the part of the radio region which can penetrate the atmosphere. Everything else in this broad electromagnetic spectrum is filtered out by the atmosphere and lost to us forever. Now, for the first time in the history of science, we have the opportunity to put a telescope in orbit about the atmosphere and expand our knowledge to the full breadth of the spectrum of electromagnetic waves, incalculably increasing our understanding of our place in the cosmos. In my view, the orbiting telescope is the greatest contribution which the space program will make to basic science in this decade.

The weather introduces a second major problem of space research, one of great scientific interest and practical importance. At the present time most of meteorology is concerned with the prediction of the course of weather activity from day to day on the basis of immediately preceding observations. But meteorologists are hampered by the existence of large blank areas in the global weather map — the poles, the major deserts, and the southern oceans — in which storms can brew undetected for days before passing out over inhabited areas. Satellites can tremendously strengthen the hand of the meteorologist by providing continuous global coverage, and seven TIROS satellites have already been launched by NASA to provide pictures of cloud cover, as the first step toward the achievement of this objective.

The TIROS satellites also contain a tiny instrument known as an infrared detector, which may be the progenitor of even more significant developments than cloud cover photography in the long run. The infrared detector measures the heat radiated from the surface and atmosphere of the planet. If this information is combined with other sources, it indicates the balance of energy in various regions of the atmosphere, which provides the driving forces for weather activity. When we have measured the atmospheric energy balances with the aid of satellites, we will know some of the causes of weather, and may make the breakthrough from 24 hour predictions to forecasts of a week or longer.

Another problem to which the space program can make a unique contribution is the question of the origin of the solar system. We know that the solar system was formed about 4.5 billion years ago, but we do not know how it was formed, and this problem has been the subject of much thought and speculation for centuries. The investigation of the early history of the solar system by instruments carried to the moon and planets in space flight vehicles is a project of the greatest scientific importance and general interest.

The moon plays a special role in this investigation because it is a body whose surface has preserved the record of its history for an exceptionally long time. On the earth, the atmosphere and the oceans wear away surface features in 10 to 50 million years. Mountain-building activity turns over large areas of the surface in about the same time. There is little left on the surface of the earth of features that existed several hundred million or a billion years ago, and the same is probably true of Mars and Venus, whose properties resemble those of the earth. But on the moon there are no oceans and atmosphere to destroy the surface, and there is little if any of the mountain-building activity which rapidly changes the face of the earth.

For these reasons the moon has retained a record of its history which probably extends back through many billions of years to the infancy of the solar system. To the student of the origin of the solar system the moon is even more important scientifically than Mars and Venus.

The internal structure of the moon can also provide clues to the origin of the solar system, quite apart from the study of its surface features. One of the theories for the formation of the planets, which was taught to me in high school and was popular until recent times, held that they were created during a near collision between our sun and another star, in which the gravitational forces between these two massive bodies tore out huge streams of flaming gas. As the second star receded, the masses of gas which happened to be near the sun were captured by it into orbits in which they eventually cooled and solidified to form the planets.

If such a collision was the way in which the solar system was formed, then the moon and the planets must have been very hot at an earlier stage in their histories. In that case, the heavy elements in their interiors would melt and run to the center to form a dense core. Iron is the most abundant of the heavy elements, and, according to this theory, all planetary bodies would therefore have iron cores.

Another theory holds that the planets were formed out of condensations of gas and dust around the sun. We know that stars themselves are probably formed in this way, by the condensation of interstellar gas and dust. It seems likely that smaller condensations would develop in the cloud of dust around the primitive sun during the early stages of its lifetime, before all the surrounding material had been drawn to the center by gravity. The moon and planets would then have been formed out of these subcondensations.

If the moon and planets were indeed condensed out of gas and dust, then the iron in their interiors would not necessarily melt and flow to the center. Planets as large as the earth might be expected to melt completely, as a result of the heating due to decay of radioactive elements in the interior, and thus to develop iron cores in any case. But the moon is smaller and colder, and if it were formed cold, enough heat would be lost from the lunar surface to keep it from melting subsequently. As a result, the moon would not form an iron core, but would retain a structure in which bits of iron are distributed through the main body of rock, like raisins in a fruitcake.

During the lunar exploration program, we hope to study this and other questions related to the internal structure of the moon, by landing on its surface instruments of the kind used to study the interior of the earth.

I have mentioned some of the scientific applications of the space program but neglected the technical problems involved in their implementation. These problems are extremely difficult, and the response to them brings out the very best efforts of the engineering community — developments which may prove to be as great an economic benefit as any of the direct applications of the program.

But there is also a negative aspect to the technological developments of space research. The engineering requirements of the space program are so advanced, and the rocket launching is so extraordinary an event in itself, that in our concern with those matters we tend to forget the purpose of all the activity. This is to put into orbit, or out into space, the package of instruments that is riding in the nose of that rocket. These instruments are the justification and the purpose of the project.

The manned program is one of the most demanding sectors of our space technology, and it also represents an extraordinary example of human courage and fortitude. Yet in our intense interest and concern with this program, we should remember that the astronaut rides in the spacecraft because, in the advanced stages of the program, he will be able to do things, by the exercise of his judgment and discrimination, which give him information that we cannot obtain by instruments alone.

The participant in manned flight can apply the accumulated wisdom of mankind to his experiences; and for that reason the manned mission represents the culminating and most rewarding phase in the exploration of the solar system.

But we must keep in mind that manned flights are not an end in themselves but only a step toward the achievement of this exploration.

At the same time the engineering developments are of vital importance because without them we achieve nothing. The engineering requirements are not straightforward, they pose extremely difficult problems, which must be surmounted in order to develop the techniques for depositing first instruments and later men on the moon. Everyone follows with the keenest interest the developments which overcome these technical obstacles, one by one, as we advance toward the achievement of our objective. But the purpose of all this is not to bring men and instruments to the moon, but rather to acquire valuable information, to extend the frontiers of our knowledge, to strengthen our control over our environment and to expand man's sensory experience and activities to other bodies of the solar system.

These are the developments which will, as in the case of the earlier voyages of discovery, reflect back on our lives and our society, bring in new scientific developments, refresh our ideas, and enlarge our perspectives. Those were the great benefits of the explorations of 500 years ago — and they will also be the enduring benefits of space exploration.

There is a tendency to forget these matters because the problems of operational responsibility for manned flight and other projects of the space program are so demanding that we may lose sight of what we are after. The eventual aim seems insignificant against the realities of the immediate pressures and the need to get things done.

Yet, if we permit ourselves to forget the importance of these objectives under the pressure of the technical problems, an atmosphere develops in which specific projects are viewed not as milestones marking progress toward permanent achievements, but each as an end in itself.

When that happens, the individual milestones, such as the manned lunar landing, come to be viewed as isolated spectaculars, and the entire program may be judged by the success or failure of one particular flight. In fact, a set of circumstances arises in which the value judgments are those of the spectacular, rather than being based on the historical record of the benefits of scientific research and exploration.

This is a serious difficulty which confronts the space program, and in order to overcome it, we must put more effort into communicating the really enduring objectives of the program — the continuing nature of the explorations, the accompanying research, and practical applications, and the indirect effects on the economy.

The problem is one of communication, primarily for NASA to solve; but it is an extremely difficult one because the rocketry and the launchings are exciting and tangible, and the most easily communicated to large numbers of people. Therefore, they are features of the space program which are stressed by the press and other important groups outside NASA.

I believe that this problem of communication, which NASA faces as a major technical agency, is related to one of the central issues of our times — and that is how to improve communications in general between scientists and the rest of society.

This is a matter which has been stressed by C. P. Snow with great effectiveness, and it is a question of deep personal concern to me and to other scientists who have been immersed in major technical programs of national significance. We see that people in public affairs, who are generally oriented towards human relationships, and have a good understanding of political and social institutions, are put off by the myth of scientific infallibility and the apparent formality of scientific arguments. Their judgment is hampered by this separation between themselves and scientists — by the feeling that scientists are a very different group of people who do not pursue their affairs in the same way as others, and who are not subject to the same limitations as the rest of us. For this reason, they do not feel able to make the same intuitive judgments of scientists as advisors, that they would make of economists, for example, whose advice they sought.

This is one of the problems that especially interests C. P. Snow, but I disagree with his analysis in one major respect. I believe that much of the burden for this gap between the cultures rests on the scientists, who like to create a jargon and a mystique which make it difficult for the non-scientist to understand either the substance of their scientific argument, or the limitations of their reasoning.

This myth of scientific truth and infallibility — the myth that science begins with a premise of established fact, proceeds through formal reasoning, and arrives in this way at an incontrovertible conclusion — is responsible for the stereotype of the scientist as a man who is divorced from his environment and functions above it in some sense. Physics is generally regarded as a difficult field, but the problems of human and political relationships are also extremely difficult; and perhaps the success of physicists is due to the simplicity and well-defined character of the problems of their work. I hope that the political education of scientists, which is now a continuing process through their increasing involvement in matters of public interest in Washington, will cause them to lose a certain degree of intellectual arrogance about the difficulty of their profession and will develop in them a degree of interest in human affairs, to the point that the scientific community will be willing to put more effort into communicating what it is doing to all of us who are very much affected by its actions.

But there is another side to the problem. Although on the one hand the scientist must become better aware of the realities of the non-scientific world and the complexities of social and political relationships, on the other hand we must try to give the non-scientist, whose primary interest is not in science but is usually in human relationships, a minimal knowledge of science so that he can make critical judgments on the basis of an understanding of all the forces, including that of science, which are at work in society.

One of the important responsibilities of our universities is the development of a kind of science education which will produce for students in law, government and other non-technical fields an understanding of some of the substance of science and the main lines of scientific enquiry, in the context of the political, social and economic developments of the times in which the principal scientific advances occurred. Most physicists still teach physics for non-scientists as though the student were going on to work in the field, with emphasis on problem-solving techniques and formal methods. Such a dehumanized presentation of physics will extinguish the interest of all but the most strongly motivated students, those who have such an overwhelming curiosity regarding the physical nature of the world that they can survive this dessicated account of the sciences. In the teaching of physics it should be understood, I think, that the person who does not propose to specialize in science is primarily interested in political and social institutions and human relationships. He needs a minimal knowledge of the substance of physics, so that he can gain a rudimentary understanding of the basic facts which enter into the determination of our way of life. But it must be presented to him in the context of other important events and names with which he is familiar and with which he can identify.

This may be the way in which to convey to the layman the main streams of thought in science. I propose that this type of presentation would be of value to the intelligent person who is not going on to work in science but still must develop his own life and make judgments on the basis of an understanding of the forces which shape his society.

In conclusion, I should like to mention a significant influence that space research is exerting on the physical sciences as a whole. The scientific areas of the space program draw on large segments of physics, astronomy and the earth sciences, which together constitute what was once called natural philosophy. The unifying element of these investigations is a general spirit of inquiry into the nature of the external physical world. It represents a redirection of interest away from the increasingly narrow specialization which has characterized the physical sciences in the last decade.

Some hint of these new elements can be seen in the people who are engaged in research in this field. For example, in the Institute for Space Studies, we have drawn together people of widely different backgrounds — from nuclear physics in my own case, for example, and from geophysics, astronomy, and applied mathematics — all of us motivated by the desire to inquire into the nature of the planets and the stars.

I believe that one can discern, as an accompaniment to this very general interest in the external world, a greater degree of outward direction, of concern with the relation of one's work to that of other people and to one's society.

And, alongside the achievements of the space program, we must place this spirit of catholicity and this redirection of interest as one of the most important consequences of science in space.

3

Leonard S. Silk

VALUES AND GOALS OF SPACE EXPLORATION

1. *Doubts about Space*

Decisions about the size and character of space programs are particularly difficult for a democratic society to make. This is so for a number of reasons: The complexity of the scientific, technical, organizational, diplomatic, national security, and even philosophical issues involved; the enormous costs of exploring and using outer space, which the people must sanction and control; the uncertainty of receiving proportionate benefits from such outlays, either in the short or long run; and the difficulties of comparing the possible costs and benefits of space programs with other government — or private — activities.

After the Soviets' electrifying success with Sputnik I in 1957, the upsweep in United States space spending encountered little drag, either from Congress or the general public. There seemed to be funds available for virtually everything anybody wanted to do in the glamorous space field. But by 1963 that phase appeared to be coming to an end; objections were rising to further steep increases in space expenditures, which in 1963 were already running above $7-billion, including both civilian and military programs. In part, this growing resistance was probably due to domestic political factors. Certain industries and regions had already benefited greatly from the heavy outflow of Federal funds for space, and pressures were building up for increased support to other groups or regions within the economy, especially with relatively high rates of unemployment persisting among the uneducated and unskilled — many of whom were Negroes. Public and Congressional critics of huge space expenditures seized upon evidence that the Soviets were opting out of a "race" to land men on the moon as justification for reining in proposed further large increases in United States space spending.

A number of influential Congressmen and Senators pointedly questioned the value of a "crash" program to put men on the moon, relative to the values of other desirable national programs in education, medical care, housing, etc. "The real question before Congress," declared Senator Fulbright in a speech that provoked widespread attention, "is one of priorities, of how we are to allocate our great but not unlimited resources among many important national programs." In fact, the problem of priorities was emerging more sharply as the public and Congressional mood turned away from large annual increases in the total Federal budget toward tax reduction as a means of stimulating a more rapid rate of economic growth and of achieving a higher level of employment. If the growth of the total Federal budget were to be more tightly controlled, it would be more difficult for space spending to grow, since this would mean diverting funds from other programs with powerful political and institutional forces to protect them from cutbacks.

There had also developed a more questioning mood among the scientific community itself over the relative priorities being given to space as compared with other research programs bidding for popular support. A number of leading scientists were questioning the emphasis upon so-called "big science" in space; their doubts were greatest about the manned moon mission. While acknowledging that much scientific and technical progress had been made in the space field, critics emphasized that space was obviously not the only goal of research and warned that space research should not be allowed to waste scientific manpower that might be better used elsewhere. The issue of how to determine priorities among particular scientific programs, and among public activities generally, promised to be with the American people for a long time to come.

Many observers — including some leading scientists — were deeply concerned over the hazards of permitting political demands to make the key decisions as to how the nation's scarce intellectual resources were to be allocated and used. Such concerns had mounted because the Federal government had come to dominate science and research to a degree no scientist would have dreamed possible only a decade ago. The year after World War II ended, the U. S. government was putting about $1-billion into research and development. By 1963 this figure had risen almost to $15-billion. This outpouring of government R & D money — over three-fourths of which was going to private industry and to educational institutions — inevitably raised questions over the extent to which government officials and their principal advisers presently control American scientific and intellectual life, and whether this might be a malign influence upon science and the nation.

Dr. James A. Van Allen, of the University of Iowa, charged that "the whole spirit of science in government has come under political pressure," particularly through what he described as the authoritarian nature of the President's Science Advisory Committee. "In matters of science," said Dr. Van Allen, "the U. S. government now exists almost wholly apart from the people." He further charged that the President's advisory committee made decisions and issued statements without considering a proper body of evidence and that scientists who appeared before the group were often so intimidated that they fell in with a popular view, with full knowledge that such a view was scientifically unwarranted.

Dr. Alvin M. Weinberg, the director of Oak Ridge National Laboratory, warned against allowing over-all U. S. science strategy, whether it involves expenditures in space or in any other field, to be settled by default, "or to be pre-empted

by the group with the most skillful publicity department."
Dr. Weinberg cautioned:

> In making our choices we should remember the ex-
> periences of other civilizations. Those cultures which
> have devoted too much of their talent to monuments
> which had nothing to do with the real issues of human
> well-being have usually fallen upon bad days: history
> tells us that the French Revolution was the bitter fruit
> of Versailles, and that the Roman Colosseum helped not
> at all in staving off the barbarians. So it is for us to
> learn well these lessons of history: we must not allow
> ourselves, by short-sighted seeking after fragile monu-
> ments of big science, to be diverted from our real pur-
> pose, which is the enriching and broadening of human
> life.

2. Space as a National Goal

Issues of our national values and goals are basic to determining what proportion of national resources we should be de-
voting to the space programs and to research generally, and
how we should allocate resources among different areas of research. The economist, as such, is better at indicating optimal
means to achieve given ends than in specifying what the ends
of economic activity should be. In our democratic society, it is
supposed to be the people who determine — both through their
dollar votes and through their political votes — what direction
the society shall take. What does the public demand of research?

I have sought an empirical answer to this key question. I
have gone out and asked a sample of the public what it *does*
demand of research.

I shall not disclose the precise size of my sample to you,
but, as any good pollster or Soviet statistician would do, I shall
report my results in percentage terms:

Of all the persons interviewed as to what they demanded
of research, 59.5% replied: "Don't know." Among my
"don't knows" I include all those people who replied, "I

don't understand what you mean." Their confusion is understandable: Can a democracy determine the aims of research?

Among the remaining 40.5% of my sample, however, I got a fascinating set of answers. In order to get them, I had to talk at great length to my respondents, clarify the question in my own way, probe and lead the witnesses hither and yon, and thereby destroy the scientific and objective nature of my survey. I cannot, therefore, give you any further precise percentage distributions of what my respondents demanded. However, among their answers (in which some people thought they were talking for the rest of the public, and some only for themselves), the following were the major themes of what my public said it demanded of research:

- Discoveries that would lead to useful inventions;
- Discoveries that would make people, business organizations, and the nation, richer;
- Scientific and technological breakthroughs that would establish our superiority over the Russians;
- Intellectual achievements that—apart from whatever the Russians did—would strengthen our pride in America;
- Findings that would cure diseases and prolong human life;
- Intellectual adventuring that would give us a more meaningful national purpose than simply more and more consumption;
- Discoveries for the sake of discoveries;
- And, finally—this from a sophisticated and rather cynical element in my sample—*entertainment*.

The views of this last element deserve somewhat more detailed reporting. Their contention was that, in the past, the public really wanted practical results from research and technology: machines to lift great weights or weave cloth or cut logs or carry people and freight or increase crop yields, etc. But such objectives applied in the era of the economics of scarcity—you will here recognize the hand of Professor Galbraith. Now the era of scarcity has given way—at least in the United States—to one of affluence; boredom or a surfeit of honey has begun to strangle the growth of a free society; capitalism is in danger of dying—as Professor Schumpeter once warned it would—of inanition. Little remains to demand of research and technology but entertainment. We have a great many intelligent and well-trained people around—and we are going to have more and more; but it is a rather foolish waste of their talents to put them to work making even faster lathes and cutting machines, etc., because all of these devices are designed either to turn out more goods—which we allegedly don't want, anyhow—or to disemploy more human labor, and the difficulties in finding work for the intellectually-inferior members of society is getting to be a bothersome enough problem as it is.

Of course, the argument runs, we might choose to make leisure for everyone the great social goal, but most people still dislike or even fear an excess of leisure, and they either grow despondent or get into trouble if you give them too much of it. This is particularly true, incidentally, of scientists and technologists, who just can't let work alone. Therefore we have devised this scientific adventure, this space exploration business, as a means of giving employment to our scientists and engineers and, at the same time, of giving entertainment to the masses, just as the Middle Ages invented the tournament to give employment to warlike knights and to provide fun and games for the people (because you simply couldn't be waging real wars all the time—that would be simply too destructive).

This new version of the Medieval tournament, the race into space and other sectors of the unknown, has, in a highly industrialized society, the added advantage of providing opportunities for industry, and thus preventing a breakdown in the existing economic, political, and social order. This might be even more important than it is today if we were ever to get an effective arms control or disarmament agreement involving substantial reductions in defense expenditures.

President Kennedy maintained that our journey into space is, if not for the purpose of entertainment (a thin word, but not one ordinarily despised by Americans), then for adventure, in response to a great challenge. In Houston, in September of 1962, the President said:

> The exploration of space will go ahead whether we join in it or not, and it is one of the great adventures of all time, and no nation which expects to be the leader of other nations can expect to stay behind in this race for space.
>
> Those who came before us made certain that this country rode the first waves of the industrial revolution, the first waves of modern invention and the first wave of nuclear power. And this generation does not intend to founder in the backwash of the coming age of space. We mean to be a part of it—we mean to lead it. . . .
>
> But why, some say, the moon? Why choose this as our goal? And they may well ask why climb the highest mountain? Why thirty-five years ago fly the Atlantic? Why does Rice play Texas?
>
> We choose to go to the moon. We choose to go to the moon.
>
> We choose to go to the moon in this decade, and do the other things, not because they are easy, but because they are hard; because that goal will serve to organize and measure the best of our energies and skills; because that challenge is one that we're willing to accept; one we are unwilling to postpone, and one we intend to win—and the others too.
>
> It is for these reasons that I regard the decision last year to shift our efforts in space from low to high gear as among the most important decisions that will be made during my incumbency in the office of the Presidency.

President Kennedy concluded by saying that, many years ago, the great British explorer George Mallory, who was to die on Mount Everest, was asked why he wanted to climb it. He said: "Because it is there." Said our late President: "Well, space is there, and we're going to climb it. And the moon and the planets are there, and new hope for knowledge, and peace are there. And therefore, as we set sail, we ask God's blessing on the most hazardous and dangerous and greatest adventure on which man has ever embarked."

In this complex century in which we live—in which total cynicism co-exists with high idealism, scientific brilliance co-exists with social stupidity—utter selfishness with dedication to all of mankind—there are those who reacted to the President's words with inspiration, and others who reacted with deep skepticism, regarding his words as a rationalization for a program undertaken for a set of political, economic, and military purposes. Pure truth in matters affecting human behavior is awfully hard, if not impossible, to come by; everyone sees reality through his own eyes, interprets it out of his own experience, images, values.

May I, then, give my own view of what we Americans demand of space research, and of scientific and technological advance more generally, since it is all part of a great and unified whole?

We live in a world still struggling for human freedom, still in danger of the most terrible destruction ever visited upon the human race.

Thus far we have preserved the peace—the imperfect peace, such as it is—through the threatened use of our military power, so dependent upon our scientific and technological prowess. An uneasy balance of terror exists in the world. But new technological breakthroughs could upset the present balance of terror; the research revolution of our time makes that a constant possibility. In fact, as Stefan Possony has said, "The rapidly accelerating technological race is the essence of the conflict. . . ." For years to come, we shall have to rely on information and intelligence systems, and on R & D work to forestall any enemy surprises in operations or in technology. This technological competition makes our laboratories and testing grounds and—alas—universities critical theaters of the world conflict. But these are also the places where the turning of the conflict into a nuclear holocaust may be prevented—where, conceivably, we may find it possible to moderate and break down the conflict itself. Space—the unfathomable ocean in which our all-too-little lifeboat of a world moves—may hold the answer to man's fate.

Space exploration is very much caught up in the swings in Soviet-United States relations. In the atmosphere of *détente* following the atmospheric nuclear test-ban treaty in 1963, President Kennedy proposed that the U.S. join the Soviet Union in an expedition to the moon. But the nation was not prepared for so sudden a proposal to convert space from a cold-war (conceivably, hot-war) zone into a theater for peaceful cooperation. In fact, it became immediately apparent that a joint Soviet-American moon venture would face formidable technical and military-security complications; cold-war considerations—and hot-war dangers—would not disappear over night.

However, one of the immediate, possibly unforeseen, effects of the President's proposal was to raise questions in the Congress about the urgency of continuing the space race to the moon against the Russians. The Administrator of NASA, James E. Webb, had the difficult and delicate job of simultaneously backing the President's proposal for Soviet-American cooperation in space, while maintaining a sense of urgency about the manned lunar expedition and, indeed, the entire space program. "Americans," said Mr. Webb, "are too sophisticated to cut off a successful program where 90 percent of the work is already under contract." A joint moon effort would not necessarily mean American and Russian astronauts would ride in the same space ships, but, he said, could start with other forms of cooperation:

The President's proposal seeks to move the United States space program and United States space philosophy to its logical, but at the same time to its most challenging, limits. It is worth emphasizing, however, that this is an extension of this basic philosophy, rather than a change in policy. . . . In itself cooperation in space activity between the great antagonists of the cold war is a thrilling, thrilling prospect. . . . But the **significance of this possibility** is not limited to space. Rather, it lies equally in the fact that cooperation in space is one more step toward cooperation on earth, toward the banishment of the fear of the annihilation of life as we know it.

Because such arguments did not not seem to be having the desired effect upon the Congress, however, Mr. Webb in succeeding weeks shifted his emphasis to the military importance of the space program and greatly scaled down the estimated costs of landing men on the moon. Although space officials had long used an estimate of $20-billion to $40-billion for the moon mission, Mr. Webb now said that the *additional* costs of the manned flight to the moon would be only $3-billion. Other space officials, produced other cost estimates—that varied chiefly because of different definitions of "additional" costs. Dr. Edward C. Welsh, executive director of the National Aeronautics and Space Council, estimated the additional cost at $7-billion. Dr. Robert C. Seamans, Jr., the NASA associate administrator, offered an estimate of $2-billion. And Dr. George Mueller, deputy administrator for manned space flight, said the extra costs of the manned lunar trip would be only $1-billion or less. The great bulk of the original cost estimates, the space officials generally agreed would have to be met, with or without putting men on the moon; they contended that only the lunar excursion model and some of the scientific investigations of the moon were directly involved and necessary for the lunar landing. The scaled-down cost estimates of the return trip to the moon obviously appealed to the Senators, who were hard pressed to justify the huge costs of the moon shot to their constituents.[1]

Despite all the confusions and shifts in the political weather, however, the United States will persist in its effort to explore and utilize space. A part of the irony of man's fate—and of his greatest adventures of the body or the mind—is that he can never escape the prison of his skin, and never escape the tangle of political and economic causes and consequences, vested interests and ideologies that are his inheritance.

It is extremely difficult really to know what draws us on. It may be, most fundamentally, man's age-old quest for knowledge. In the words of Professor George Sarton:

> The history of science is the story of a protracted struggle, which will never end, against the inertia of superstition and ignorance, against the liars and hypocrites, against the deceivers and the self-deceived, against all the forces of darkness and nonsense. . . . Science develops very much as if it had a life of its own. Great social events cast their shadows before and after upon science as well as upon other human activities; and however alive and independent science may ever be, it never develops in a political vacuum. Yet each scientific question suggests irresistibly new questions connected with it by no bonds but the bonds of logic. Each new discovery exerts as it were a pressure in a new direction, and causes the growth of a new branch of science, or at least a new twig. The whole fabric of science seems thus to be growing like a tree; in both cases the dependence upon the environment is obvious enough, yet the main cause of growth — the growth pressure, the urge to grow—is inside the tree, not outside. Thus science is as it were independent of particular people, though it may be affected at sundry times

---

[1] John W. Finney, "Estimate of Cost of Moon Trip Cut," *New York Times* October 18, 1963, p. 1.

by each of them. The tree of science symbolizes the genius and the glory of mankind as a whole.[2]

We will surely not turn back from our effort to explore outer space. But the scope and pace of the effort will obviously be determined by many social, political and economic factors.

3. *Economic Consequences*

On the assumption that we do continue to maintain a high level of expenditures for space research and exploration, what will be the consequences for our national economy? So great are the technical, scientific, and political uncertainties that only a charlatan would pretend to give a very tight prediction, but I believe that some meaningful statements about the probable economic effects of our space programs can be made on the basis of what we already know.

There will be some significant technological benefits to the civilian economy, resulting from the "spin-off" of space research. The most obvious immediate example is that of international communications systems, based on earth satellites. Existing cost and demand projections make such systems look like not only a good bet for the new communications company, but virtually a necessity if the world is to achieve the degree of integration conducive to optimal economic development as well as to social and political stability. Weather satellites also promise real benefits to business decision-making and planning in many areas. In addition, there should be a continuing stream of other innovations in new materials, such as dry-film lubricants, ceramics and metals; paints and coatings; more effective shielding materials, such as pyrolytic graphite; new methods of metal fabrication and forming, such as the technique of explosive forming; new or improved power and propulsion forces, especially small nuclear-electric generating systems; new biological applications, affecting medicine,

---

[2] George Sarton, *The History of Science and the New Humanism,* George Braziller, Inc., New York, 1956, pp. 177-178.

food processing, air purification, control of temperature and humidity, etc.; electronic applications—for instance, involving new uses of masers and lasers.

It is well, however, to be cautious in predicting the speed with which innovations are absorbed into the civilian economy. In some cases, the applications may take only a few years, in others a few decades. The most important consequences may indeed be a long time coming. It would seem to me, however, that over time the advances that are being achieved in so many fields—physics, chemistry, biology, electronics, electrical engineering, mechanical engineering—are bound to permeate our entire industrial organism.

The Denver Research Institute, in the most comprehensive study that has thus far been done on the technological transfers to the civilian economy from missile and space programs,[3] identifies 33 broad technological areas in which transfers have occurred or can be reasonably expected to occur in the future. The report describes 185 transfer examples—by no means all that were found. These, the Denver investigators concluded, provide evidence of the magnitude, scope and nature of the technological transfers that have already occurred. They believe, however, that, due to inevitable time lags and the relative recency of major space outlays, "most of the transfer is still to occur."

The Denver group attaches less importance to the direct transfer of particular *products* from missile/space programs than to the transfer of *technology*.

Obviously, space research is only one contributor to our vast store of technological knowledge. So complex is the transfer process—and, in some cases, so difficult is it to identify—

---

[3] *The Commercial Application of Missile/Space Technology,* Parts 1 and 2, Denver Research Institute, University of Denver, September, 1963. This study was based on information obtained during January-October, 1962, from interviews with 360 persons in 189 organizations and from 988 responses to questionnaires sent to 3,507 organizations. The organizations surveyed were largely industrial firms.

that the Denver investigators believe that it is not feasible to measure in quantitative terms the impact of space technology on the commercial sector of the economy. They observe that "insufficient understanding of the nature of the transfer process appears to have been one reason for widely divergent views on the past and future importance of missile/space contributions to commercially useful technology."

Nevertheless, it is fair to say that technological transfers from space and military research have been occurring at a slower pace than the public had been led to expect. If such transfers are to be facilitated, it will be necessary to improve mechanisms for linking new technological knowledge with market requirements information. However, the impediments to technological transfer are much greater than just a lack of market information. The real problem is overcoming the social, economic, and institutional resistances that make the absorption process a slow one. Among the most serious types of resistances are those of unemployment and vested interests in existing technologies, on the part of both labor and management.

There has recently been a tendency to question the social and economic value of technological progress stemming from research and development because of the apparent failure of the national economy to achieve more rapid growth during the years while R & D expenditures were rapidly rising.[4] But to criticize R & D on such grounds is to attack a straw man. The increase in scientific and technical knowledge resulting from R & D is only one factor in determining the economic performance of a nation. In the short run, the positive impact of new knowledge and technological change may be curbed by other economic or social factors—especially by the

---

[4] See Robert A. Solo, "Gearing Military R & D to Economic Growth," Harvard Business Review, November-December, 1962. For a critique of the Solo article, see W. H. Gruber "What Can We Expect from our New Economy?", School of Industrial Management, Massachusetts Institute of Technology, September, 1963.

inadequacy of aggregate demand and the relative immobility of parts of the labor force. It would be foolish to expect higher productivity, in and of itself, quickly to create full employment and faster overall growth.

In fact, the short-run impact of R & D upon an economy may be somewhat like the new steroid drugs which can either cause temporary sterility or lead to greatly increased fertility, depending on the timing of the doses and the state of the organism when it receives them.

Over the longer run, there can be no doubt that the "fertility" effects are of major importance; economic growth, as study after study has shown, significantly derives from the expansion of scientific and technological knowledge, culminating in new products, new processes, new resources. The improvement in human skills and ability—closely related to the growth of knowledge—is also a critical element in the economic growth process. But, of course, the growth process is a complex one, involving many other economic, social, and institutional factors.

Research and development carried on in connection with the space program will contribute to long-term economic growth. It will do this through the types of effects identified in the Denver Research Institute study—that is, through (1) the stimulation of basic and applied research; (2) the development of new or improved processes and techniques; (3) the improvement of existing products; (4) the increased availability of materials, testing equipment, and laboratory equipment; (5) the development of new products; and (6) through cost reduction. Such contributions of space research promise to augment the historical impact of scientific and technological progress upon output, income, and employment in the Western world. The growth of knowledge and the force of technical innovation has provided the answer to Karl Marx and other pessimists who expected the capitalist process to create a steadily growing "reserve army of the unemployed," an embittered and impoverished proletariat that would finally rise up and overthrow the small number of capitalists who controlled the means of production.

But, as Simone de Beauvior has said of Count Donatien de Sade, must we burn Marx? Or, rather, can we? Marx was, after all, no Luddite. He was, on the contrary, well aware of the power of capitalism to expand by employing modern and superior technology; and he despised those sentimentalists and reactionaries who would turn the clock back toward feudalism. Further, Marx thought of himself as a scientific observer of economic reality. And what he saw of the process of industrial change, resulting from new technology, was anything but smooth or continuously benign in its immediate effect upon the welfare of the workers.

Marx saw the entire structure of industry and of the labor force being metamorphosed by new technology. Studying the Census of England and Wales, he noted that, from 1851 to 1861, employment had dropped in agriculture, worsted manufacture, silk-weaving, hat-making, straw-hat and bonnet-making, chandlery, comb-making, nail-making and other lines. But in coal mining and cotton spinning and weaving, Marx observed that there had been huge increases in employment. "The increase of laborers is generally greatest since 1851," he concluded, "in such branches of industry in which machinery has not up to the present been employed with success." Substituting different dates and industries, we can give this passage current relevancy. In fact, we must try to update Marx by considering the possible disruptions that may result from the substitution of new technology for either labor or capital— and how these disruptions may be reduced and overcome. Admittedly, the disruptions may be transitory phenomena. But they can still be painful for people caught in them, and even more difficult to overcome because of the greater barriers to occupational mobility that are created by higher requirements for education and skills.

Rapid transition to new technologies may also be painful for society as a whole, because all of the growth-stimulative effects of innovation may, under the wrong circumstances, be growth-arresting. Innovations which increase productivity may displace workers and breed unemployment—if aggregate demand in the economy does not expand sufficiently to create jobs for the displaced workers. And that unemployment will itself increase the drags upon economic growth. Innovations in the form of new products may kill off the demand for old products and leave workers stranded and jobless—if those workers, for lack of education, skills, trade union rules, or other reasons are incapable of moving to those job opportunities which are developing. Innovations in equipment accelerate the obsolescence of existing capital goods and may also breed excess capacity—and thus arrest growth. Resource innovations may leave the region producing the "old" resources desolate unless a new use can be found for its resources, or unless its institutions (especially its educational institutions) can be transformed, to make possible renewed life.

Thus, there is no reason to assume that the income-generating effects of innovation—resulting from space research or any other—must automatically match or exceed the displacement effects of innovation on labor, capital, or other resources. Nor can we assume that the wage and price system of an economy automatically works promptly to attract labor and other resources from contracting to expanding industries. The mobility of our human or material resources may be further impeded by many types of influence—monopolistic or oligopolistic barriers, habits or fears that inhibit geographical or occupational mobility, ignorance of markets, and all the other ways in which an economy, or parts of it, are cramped and muscle-bound.

One of the most painful social adjustments forced by space developments is in the area of brainpower. Some programs have already greatly increased the demand for highly-trained professional and technical personnel and have created a problem of technological obsolescence among our older scientists and engineers. This technological obsolescence, as

Dean Gordon S. Brown of the M.I.T. School of Engineering sees it, is at the base of our chronic shortage of high-quality personnel.[5] Dean Brown has pointed out that few engineers trained earlier than 1950 received adequate preparation for many fields, including modern atomic and nuclear physics, and nuclear engineering; feed-back control, automation, and inertial guidance; information theory and advanced theories of communications; modern computer technology which penetrates into engineering analysis and design; solid-state physics and molecular engineering, with their impact on the era of solid-state electronics; the exploitation of superconductivity and other properties of modern materials; plasma physics, which plays an important role in the development of techniques for space propulsion, and has potential for new forms for energy conversion; computer-aided design and numerical control of machine tools, which may increase the production capabilities of industry; modern treatment of the interactions of electro-magnetic theory with fluid dynamics, with statistical and wave mechanics; probability theory and its role in engineering decision-making; relativity theory; modern mathematics; and the extra-terrestrial sciences. Although many of these areas of science and technology have become professional disciplines of major scope, with great significance for our military posture and technological strength, a significant majority of practicing engineers and engineering teachers—still considered young men—left college, as Dean Brown notes, before most of these disciplines were even visualized—and before the scientific bases upon which they rest were taught efficiently.

Beyond doubt, the types of knowledge and skills required for so great a space effort as is presently envisioned will mean a great impact upon our educational institutions. This will intensify problems of governmental involvement in education

---

[5] Gordon S. Brown, "Closing the Engineering Gap," *The Technology Review*, Volume LXV, Number 8, June 1963, Massachusetts Institute of Technology, Cambridge, Mass.

in both our public and private schools and colleges and universities. It will also intensify the problem of making wise choices in how we allocate scarce intellectual resources to all the areas of science, social science, the humanities, politics and government, business, labor, and other occupations.

Space activities are sometimes thought of by the public as demanding much money but few people. This is wrong. Space work is highly labor-intensive, with more jobs created per dollar of expenditure than most other industries, such as autos, steel, or petroleum, with their longer production runs and heavier capital costs.[6] A RAND study suggests that in 1970, total projected space expenditures of $13-billion would imply jobs for 528,000 persons employed by prime contractors alone. Additional jobs created among subcontractors and suppliers should more than double that number.

Indeed, space has impressive qualifications as an industrial civilization's equivalent of pyramid-building. The space effort could provide a substitute for a part of our huge military outlays, should it become possible to scale these down appreciably in the future. Some will regard this as a boon that will enable the United States to avoid serious dislocations or unemployment that might result from disarmament. Others will regard this as an unfortunate temptation (to both industry and labor) and a guarantee that our "mixed" or "compound" economy will continue to have a large and growing sector that is dominated by government, financed out of taxes, and existing in large measure outside the choices and discipline of the free market. Some will see this as damaging the overall efficiency and growth of our economy. But others will argue, as Edward Welsh has done, that "the economic benefits for a viable space program tend to make it self-supporting through its stimulating effect upon the economy over a period of time."

---

[6] See L. S. Silk, "The Impact on The American Economy," in *Outer Space: Prospects for Man and Society*, Lincoln P. Bloomfield, ed., Prentice-Hall, Englewood Cliffs, N. J., 1962, pp. 74-75.

There can be no doubt that space raises extremely important systemic questions; we have moved a long way from the time when Adam Smith's "divine hand" could invisibly regulate our economic process through the interactions of myriads of decisions made by small consumers and producers. General Electric's Ralph Cordiner has declared that space, like national defense, will necessarily require "a close partnership" between the federal government and private industry, but that this does not imply any basic change in our system beyond what we have already experienced:

> Each of the partners must perform its appropriate role, and the problems and delays occur where government tries to do the managerial and technical work for which industry is best qualified, or industry tries to take on the functions of government.

Going much further, Professor Wassily Leontief has argued that a greater degree of planning and business-government integration will be necessary:

> The nature of advanced modern technology is such that it cannot be exploited economically without effective, sometimes ruthless, overall coordination. Such coordination must affect not only operations within a single plant, but also the relationship between plants within an industry and of all industries within a national economy as a whole. Supra-national cooperation and coordination becomes more and more necessary for efficient functioning of the individual national economies as well.

Anyone who broods very much about space developments will, I believe, begin to get some sense of the stresses and problems that are going to continue to affect the United States in the years ahead. Whether this embryo becomes a creature of joy and excitement and benefit to mankind or whether it becomes a monstrosity that needs to be chained up remains to be determined. It will depend, not upon the blind operation of that mythical being variously called History or The Future, but upon the decisions that reasonable men in a still free society are capable of making.

4. *Determining Priorities*

Making the right decisions is not going to be easy. We need better political mechanisms for evaluating proposed government programs and for setting national priorties.

Within the Administration, these functions head up to the President. He has the Bureau of the Budget to help him in shaping his overall program, together with many advisers and agency heads to explain and defend particular programs. In the area of science policy, the President now has the Office of Science and Technology to help set scientific priorities and to coordinate the government's diffuse R & D program. This is not to say that the machinery for decision-making within the Administration is (or ever can be) completely adequate to the job; government today is a huge and complex process, and political and institutional pressures, together with the changing values and needs of the times, inevitably defy any completely rational, objective, and orderly cost-effectiveness calculus and choice of the best mix of government programs—and of which activities are better left to the private economy. However hard the Administration may struggle to set priorities wisely, it requires competent criticism and reaction from the outside— especially from Congress.

In Congress, however, the situation is worse than it is within the Administration. Congress is not well set up or equipped to analyze the Federal budget as a whole, weighing the costs and benefits of individual programs in relation to each other and shaping the entire program to meet national goals. Particular programs are fought for by special-interest groups and individuals, and the job of reviewing the Administration's program is parceled out among a number of committees. Students of Congress have pointed out that Congress, with relatively few extremely busy legislative assistants, is at an enormous disadvantage with the Administration's agencies, which have sizable staffs to justify the requests for appropriations. Congress has, of course, well-tried but rather blind methods for controlling expenditures it does not understand: Refusal to change expenditures radically from past years (which Robert Wallace [7] has called the "institutionalizing of mistakes"), meat-ax cuts (which may chop off programs of value together with programs of little value), and attacks on "overhead."

Congress itself, despite its awareness of its lack of professional advice to match that of the executive branch's experts, has been slow to acquire the staff aides it needs to do a competent critical evaluation job. Some critics assert that this is because the appropriations committees in Congress oppose too great a role for professionals, fearing that their own power would be diminished. Studies by professionals would be made available to the whole Congress—and to the nation, and might lead to justification for reductions in programs which committees (especially their chairmen) favor, or to justifications for increased expenditures on programs that they want to cut. As things stand, Congress and the nation must rely heavily on the judgment of key Congressmen, who preside over particular demesnes; there are reasons for questioning whether the special power held by key members of committees is power exercised for the nation as a whole. Special interests—whose influence can in many ways be brought to bear more effectively upon Congressmen than upon the Administration—tend to be more concentrated and more powerful than general interests. Nevertheless, Congress does sometimes grow greatly exercised over particular programs that appear to be going wrong and strives to do an effective critical job to determine whether such programs are truly in the public interest.

In the broad area of research and development, over which so much uncertainty and confusion exist, Congress has now

[7] R. A. Wallace, *Congressional Control of Federal Spending*, Wayne State University Press, 1960.

launched an investigation of how the billions of public dollars are being spent and of whether this R & D activity (including the space programs) is worth the cost. Such an investigation can do much good or much harm, depending on how it is conducted. If Congressional investigators succumb to the temptation to run an old-style political probe—intended only to prove that billions have been wasted on outlandish studies— it may inflict serious damage upon the nation by choking off valuable research. But if Congressional investigators insist on an adequate budget, employ a competent staff, and do their homework, they can contribute enormously to the nation's understanding of the research revolution. They also can help devise better means of deriving social benefits from research programs.

Obviously, the task of determining national priorities cannot be put upon Congress and the Administration alone; it belongs to the people generally. And the job of educating the people on these difficult problems imposes special responsibilities upon professionally competent groups and individuals, including physical and social scientists, teachers, editors, writers, as well as upon our political leaders. We urgently need a better informed electorate to guide public policies more wisely.

We must seek to build our public policies upon deeper and more complete knowledge. We need to know more about the true costs (not only the dollar costs but the human costs) of undertaking large space programs vis-a-vis other public or private activities; and we need to know more about the real (and prospective) benefits of such programs. We need to see that realizing the benefits of research and development activities involves not only setting up better communication between researchers and industrialists but adopting many other public policies to promote the growth and welfare of the society. We must develop the budget and fiscal policies, the educational program, the resource and mobility programs that will facilitate the spread of new knowledge and technologies

—and translate these into higher per capita income, more and better jobs, and a more secure nation. All this we must seek to do in ways that will protect, and hopefully expand, our personal and political freedom, as well as our economic well-being.

5. New Aims

It might be said that the reason both the U.S. and the USSR are in the process of reappraising their space programs is that their motivation in embarking upon space research was primarily one of prestige. For the U.S., at least, the idea that we were in a race with the Russians has been the surest way to get public support for the program.

In reappraising our space program one of the first things we will have to do is define the aims of the program more clearly. This will not be easy. The whole concept of government sponsorship of a peacetime venture into the unknown with no clear end in sight is without precedent. Even the multi-billion dollar Marshall Program of the early post World War II years, a revolutionary program for the government at that time, was a program with a definite purpose—the reconstruction of war torn Europe—and with a forseeable end. The purpose of the space program, on the other hand, is amorphous and the end of it is as limitless as the universe.

Amorphous though the purpose of the space program may be, it is a purpose which has motivated mankind since the beginning of time. It is no more nor less than the pursuit of knowledge and the transfer of this knowledge into ways of improving the life of man.

Sometimes Americans gain conviction that something they are doing is right only after others follow them. The United States should therefore find some reassurance in the determination of many European industrial and political leaders to participate in a larger way in space research.

Most of the European countries have conducted research in space, particularly during and since the International Geophysical Year, although some have even longer histories of space activities.[8] Their motivation for embarking on space programs has not been one of prestige, but of survival. As Jean Delorme, President of Air Liquide, France, has said, "Unless European countries want to become backward economies within fifty years, underdeveloped in comparison with the Big Two, they must lose no time in entering this laboratory of the future. It is a question of survival. We are scientifically prepared to tackle space problems."

While most countries have their own national programs —largely connected with the less expensive type of experiments with sounding rockets—these countries realized that they could not individually compete with the U.S. or the Soviet Union.

Late in 1960 plans were made to form a European Space Research Organization (ESRO). Twelve countries—Austria, Belgium, Denmark, Germany, France, Italy, Netherlands, Norway, Spain, Sweden, Switzerland, and the United Kingdom—formed ESRO to promote collaboration among each other in space research and technology. An eight year program was set up which envisaged the launching of 440 sounding rockets; 22 small earth satellites; 8 deep space probes; 2 stabilized astronomical satellites and 2 moon satellites.

During 1961 the idea of developing a European Space Launcher was discussed in detail. By November a draft convention had been prepared to set up the European Launcher Development Organization (ELDO). The object of ELDO is to develop a heavy launcher capable of putting satellites into orbit for scientific and commercial purposes. The program calls for a first firing of a completed 3-stage launcher from Woomera, Australia towards the end of 1965, when a satellite test vehicle will be placed in orbit. The first ELDO launcher will use the British Blue Streak as its first stage, an adaptation of the French Veronique at its second stage and a third stage

---

[8] For research on European space activities, I am indebted to Mrs. M. Louise Curley.

rocket to be developed under German direction. Nine countries—Australia, Belgium, Denmark, France, Germany, Italy, Netherlands, Spain and the United Kingdom—have joined together in the formation of ELDO.

Shortly after the formation of ESRO and ELDO, European industrial interests created a non-profit-making association called EUROSPACE. The founder members were 46 companies or trade associations from Belgium, France, Germany, Italy, Netherlands, Switzerland and the United Kingdom. As of July, 1963, Sweden and Norway have also joined and there are now some 125 companies and trade associations. The companies listed as active members have a combined sales volume of $14 billion and a total labor force of over 2 million.

In effect, EUROSPACE membership comprises most of the aircraft industries, a good part of the electronic firms, the main chemicals and metals companies and many leading specialists in precision mechanics and public works in the nine member countries. In addition, most of the big European banks are corresponding members, as are eight U.S. aerospace firms.

The purpose of EUROSPACE is to ensure that European industry maintains and ultimately extends its footing in astronautics. A EUROSPACE publication, "Proposals for a European Space Program," written by 400 European scientists and economists was released in March of 1963.

Among the proposals were two for communications-satellite networks which could be set in orbit by 1968 without any assistance from the U.S. Both plans rely completely on European missiles and other equipment. For the actual communications network they would use the ELDO Rocket. All design, building and launching of the satellites would be done by Europeans. In addition to these proposals, there are others for time-keeping and navigational-aid satellites, work on new launchers and the construction of an all-European launching base somewhere along the equator.

The cost of the program is estimated at $720 million for the first four years. Over an eight year period the cost of the communications satellites alone is estimated at $773 million. The EUROSPACE nations have already allocated a total of $200 million for the ELDO rocket and $100 million for ESRO's space probes over a period of four years. In addition French and British national space programs are estimated at about $80 million. Adding the cost of the EUROSPACE program of $720 million for the first four years to the amounts allocated to ESRO and ELDO and the national space programs the total comes to $1.1 billion. This amount is some 13% of the U.S. expenditures, actual and projected, for the period 1962-65. However, it is more than one-third of the amount of U.S. outlays for unmanned vehicles. The magnitude of the European programs suggest the emergence of still another space power.

The real significance of the European space effort lies not so much in its magnitude as in its motivation. As stated earlier, these nations have embarked upon space research for survival. They firmly believe that if they opt out of the space effort they will in a sense opt out of history.

The importance of technology to economic growth has long been recognized but the relationship between the two has not been well understood. The technological process has until recently been treated as an "outside" factor in the economic process. The realization that it is an integral factor is only beginning to be felt. In a provocative study, *Scarcity & Growth*, Harold J. Barnett and Chandler Morse have written:

> A strong case can be made for the view that the cumulation of knowledge and technological progress is automatic and self-reproductive in modern economies, and obeys a law of increasing returns. Every cost-reducing innovation opens up possibilities of application in so many new directions that the stock of knowledge, far from being depleted by new developments may even expand geometrically. Technological

progress, instead of being the adventitious consequence of lucky and highly improbable discoveries, appears to obey what Myrdal has called the "principle of circular and cumulative causation," namely, that change tends to induce further change in the same direction.

The transformation of materials into final goods has become increasingly a matter of chemical processing. It is more and more rare for materials to be transformed into final products solely by mechanical means. The natural resource building blocks are now to a large extent atoms and molecules. Nature's input should now be conceived as units of mass and energy, not acres and tons. Now the problem is more one of manipulating the available store of iron, magnesium, aluminum, carbon, hydrogen and oxygen atoms, even electrons. This has major economic significance. *It changes radically the natural resources factor of production for societies that have access to modern technology and capital.* (Italics mine.)

It is the realization that the technological process is an integral part of the economic process that is basic to the European venture into space and it is this realization which will in the final analysis determine the future of the U.S. space program. To say this is not to predict clear sailing for the U.S. space program. But it does alter the framework of the argument. It takes the space effort out of the exotic and brings it into everyday life. The full employment of the technological process is as important a goal of economic policy as the full employment of men and physical resources.

Rapid scientific and technological advance in our time is having a tremendous impact upon our political and economic institutions. Some people apparently react to this rapid scientific advance with doubt and anxiety, if not fear and trembling. Yet it is possible that the greatest benefit of the space venture may eventually be a revival of optimism about man's future. As C. P. Snow has said, "They (the scientists) are inclined to be impatient to see if something can be done, until it's proved otherwise. That is their real optimism, and it's an optimism that the rest of us badly need."

To justify such optimism, however, we shall have to be as imaginative, flexible, and creative in the areas of political and social organization as we have been in science and technology.

man's future. As C. P. Snow has said, "They" (the scientists) are inclined to be impatient to see if something can be done, until it is proved otherwise. That is their real optimism, and it's an optimism that the rest of us badly need."

To justify such optimism, however, we shall have to be as imaginative, flexible, and creative in the areas of political and social organization as we have been in science and technology.

4

Horace P. Moulton

COMMERCIAL SPACE COMMUNICATIONS*

Nine years ago Dr. John R. Pierce of Bell Telephone Laboratories detailed the scientific feasibility of placing microwave stations in orbit thousands of miles in outer space where they would be visible to stations on the ground at points on different continents.[1] In this way, very broadband microwave beams could be sent from one ground station to a satellite and relayed to another ground station in another hemisphere. The ground stations would be connected to the terrestrial communications networks just as international cables and high frequency radio facilities are today.

The advantages of such a system were clear. Another high capacity facility useful for all international communications purposes could be added to the existing system to meet the ever-growing demands for more and more circuits and,

---

* Based in part on a paper presented at the 1963 Southeastern Regional Meeting of the American Society of International Law, on Feb. 2, 1963 at Chapel Hill, N.C. See "Some Legal Aspects of International Communications," 41 N.C.L. Rev. 354 (Spring 1963).

[1] Dr. Pierce's suggestions were evolved in a series of science fiction articles and were ultimately set forth in detail in "Orbital Radio Relays," a technical paper written in Nov. 1954 and published in the April 1955 issue of Jet Propulsion, at 153-57. The idea of using satellites for communications, however, appears to have been first advanced by Arthur C. Clarke, a British science writer, in an article which appeared in The Wireless World in 1945. See Pierce, "Satellite Science and Technology," the annual Halley Lecture delivered at Oxford University, 141 *Science* 237 (July 19, 1963).

in addition, to provide high quality television transmission.[2] At the time Dr. Pierce wrote, however, no satellite had flown and no rocket existed to fly one. Nor was the communications art refined to the point where an operational microwave station could be maintained in a space craft thousands of miles in the sky.

So rapid was the scientific development, however, that by early 1961 it was apparent the technical problems would soon be solved and a world-wide commercial communications satellite system could be established in a matter of a relatively few years. The first peaceful commercial use of space was thus within our grasp and the United States was far ahead in this technology. Suddenly the establishment of a world-wide space communications system under United States leadership became a matter of urgent public importance. And it

---

[2] It should be emphasized that none of the satellite systems which are presently contemplated will be used for broadcasting directly to home television receivers. See "Draft Proposals of U.S.A. for the Extraordinary Administrative Radio Conference for Space Radio communication (Geneva, 1963)," Oct. 22, 1962, at 4: "Recent experimental programs have demonstrated the technical feasibility of relaying aural and television broadcast program material via communication satellite stations. However, these demonstrations consisted of transmissions to special receiving stations on the earth's surface from which the program material was distributed over conventional terrestrial communication systems to the broadcasting stations which serve the general public. . . . Studies indicate that there is little likelihood of the general public receiving direct broadcasts from satellites in the near future. The proposals of the U.S.A. do not include provision for a broadcasting satellite service." The final United States Proposals, adopted June 1, 1963, recommend (p. 6) consideration of this subject at some future conference.

For an appraisal of the practical uses of communications satellites, see Johnson, "The Commercial Uses of Communication Satellites," 5 Calif. Management Rev. 55 (Spring 1963) and Jaffee and Smith, "The Impact of Communications Satellites on the Less Developed Areas," a paper submitted at the UN Conference on the Application of Science and Technology for Benefit of the Less Developed Areas, Agenda L.5.2 (Geneva, Jan. 1963).

was then that the great debate began.[3] From the outset it was clear that for the reasonably foreseeable future there could be only one commercial communications satellite system. So the basic issue was: What entity or group should represent the total United States interest in this undertaking?

Many proposals were advanced.[4] Seemingly endless Congressional committee hearings ensued,[5] tripping on each other's heels, so that some were reminded of Alice's Walrus when he complained to the eager little bright-faced oysters, "We cannot do with more than four to give a hand to each." A small group of Senators mounted a full-blown filibuster

---

[3] For the events leading up to the enactment of the Communications Satellite Act of 1962, see Moulton, "Communication Satellites—the Proposed Communications Satellite Act of 1962," 18 Bus. Law. 173, 174-75 (1962).

[4] For a discussion of the proposals advanced to the FCC see Moulton, op. cit. supra, n.3 at 175-76. Thereafter, 16 bills were introduced in the 2d Session of the 87th Congress, exclusive of those offered as amendments in the nature of substitutes. See 41 N.C.L. Rev. 354, 355 n.4. Interest, however, centered on four of these: the Administration's proposal (introduced as the Kerr-Magnuson bill, S. 2814, which provided for the creation of a private corporation with two classes of stock, voting stock to be owned by anyone including carriers and non-voting stock which was limited to communications carriers); the Kerr bill, S. 2650 (which provided for carrier ownership); and the Kefauver bill, S. 2890 (which provided for government ownership). S. 2814 was amended by the Senate Aeronautical and Space Sciences Committee, S. Rep. No. 1319 (April 2, 1962), and as reported was introduced as a fourth alternative in the House by Rep. Harris as H.R. 11040, the bill which eventually became law.

[5] Four committees held hearings on the proposed legislation: the Senate Aeronautical and Space Sciences Committee on Feb. 27, 28, March 1, 5, 6, and 7, 1962 (S. Rep. No. 1319, April 2, 1962); the House Interstate and Foreign Commerce Committee on March 13, 14, 15, 16, 20, 21, and 22, 1962 (H. Rep. No. 1636, April 24, 1962); the Senate Commerce Committee on April 10, 11, 12, 13, 16, 24, and 26, 1962 (S. Rep. No. 1584, June 11, 1962); and the Senate Foreign Relations Committee on Aug. 3, 6, 7, 8, and 9, 1962 (S. Rep. No. 1873, Aug. 10, 1962). In addition, hearings on related matters were held during the 87th Congress by eight committees or subcommittees. See 41 N.C.L. Rev. at 355-56 n.5.

which ended in cloture on August 14, 1962.[6] Then, at long last, the Communications Satellite Act of 1962 was enacted by overwhelming votes in both houses of Congress and became law on August 31, 1962.[7]

Section 305 of that Act authorized the creation of a private corporation whose stated purposes are to plan, construct and operate, by "itself or in conjunction with foreign governments or business entities, a commercial communications satellite system" and to "furnish for hire channels of communication to the United States communication common carriers and to other authorized entities, foreign and domestic."[8]

In the midst of this Congressional turmoil, TELSTAR arose into outer space to prove what had been assumed but never before achieved—that broadband satellite communication between continents is both possible and practical. On July 10, 1962, TELSTAR was placed in an elliptical orbit with an apogee of 3501.8 statute miles and a perigee of 593.35 statute miles.[9] The legal problems involved in TELSTAR were both mundane and ethereal. For example, we gave serious consideration to the legal liabilities attending a faulty launching which might cause the rocket and its space craft payload to fall on a place such as Miami Beach at the height of its season. We also considered the legal implications of

---

[6] The vote on cloture was 63 to 27. 108 Cong. Rec. 15398-99 (daily ed.). For a brief consideration of the basic issues involved in the debates see Brynes, "TVA in Space," The New Republic, p. 11 (July 2, 1962).

[7] Pub. L. No. 87-624, 76 Stat. 419, 47 U.S.C.A. § 701. The Senate passed the bill on Aug. 17, 1962 by a vote of 66 to 11 (108 Cong., Rec. 15874 (daily ed.)), and the House concurred on Aug. 27, 1962 by a vote of 372 to 10 (108 Cong. Rec. 16604-15 (daily ed.)).

[8] 76 Stat. 425, § 305(a), 47 U.S.C.A. § 735(a).

[9] It is anticipated that satellites actually used in a commercial system, however, will operate in substantially higher orbits. TELSTAR II, *e.g.*, which was launched on May 7, 1963 has an apogee of 6713 s.m. and a perigee of 604 s.m. As to the possible orbital configurations of a commercial system see the testimony of M. J. Stoller of NASA before the Senate Committee on Aeronautical and Space Sciences on Communications Satellite Legislation, 87th Cong., 2d Sess., 34-75 (Feb. 27, 1962).

the fact that TELSTAR once in orbit would pass over nearly every foreign nation extant.

We took comfort from the resolution of the General Assembly of the United Nations on December 20, 1961 commending that international law applies to outer space and celestial bodies and that "outer space and celestial bodies are free for exploration and use by all states in conformity with international law and are not subject to national appropriation." [10] This resolution, important as it was, obviously constituted an uncertain step forward since it made no attempt to go beyond these two broad principles or to define just where airspace ends and outer space begins, a subject upon which a rather wide range of opinion has been expressed by scholars in this field.

Most importantly, both the United States and Russia had on numerous occasions placed in orbit space vehicles flying over countries throughout the world at altitudes from hundreds to thousands of miles. For the most part, these had been experimental and scientific in character and had given rise to no protest. Thus a body of precedents was even then building for the proposition that outer space is free for all to use for peaceful purposes. Once in orbit, TELSTAR would apparently then be well above any reasonable vertical claim of sovereignty, would be used solely for peaceful purposes, and would not otherwise threaten the security or other legitimate interest of any country. Since TELSTAR's launching, no foreign voice has been raised in protest although many have been heard in acclaim. Against this background it seems that the law of space, as it evolves, will present no obstacle to the establishment of a world-wide commercial satellite communications system.

International arrangements pertaining to the allocation of frequencies for communications satellites must, of course, be made just as similar arrangements have been made in the

---

[10] U.N. Res. 1721 (XVI).

past for the use of high frequency radio facilities. Historically, these arrangements have been worked out through the offices of the International Telecommunication Union and have been embodied in international conventions. In October, 1963, an Extraordinary Administrative Radio Conference (EARC) of the ITU began in Geneva, Switzerland, and among the matters considered was the allocation of frequencies for satellite communications. Intensive preparations for this conference took place. "Draft Proposals" were formulated and circulated to all interested parties within the United States,[11] and on June 1, 1963 the "Proposals of the United States" were approved by the Department of State and transmitted to the Secretary-General of the ITU. Other nations, including Russia, submitted their own Proposals. The U.S. delegation to the conference was headed by Mr. Joseph H. McConnell as Chairman, Ambassador Jacob D. Beam as Vice Chairman and former FCC Commissioner T.A.M. Craven as Technical Chairman. The delegation also consisted of representatives of the Satellite Corporation, the communications carriers and industry generally, as well as representatives from all of the interested governmental agencies.

The Tenth Plenary Assembly of the International Radio Consulting Committee (CCIR) of the ITU, which was concluded earlier in 1963, took an important step forward when agreement was reached on many basic issues, including the feasibility of, and technical standards for, the sharing of frequencies by space systems and terrestrial services.[12] There is good reason to believe that frequency allocation questions will be resolved in an equally satisfactory manner and will not impede the establishment of a communications satellite system.[12a]

----

[11] Paglin, "The Establishment of Satellite Communications Systems," 70 Pub. Util. Fort. 606, 609-13 (Oct. 25, 1962).

[12] See Joachim, "Technical Results of the CCIR's Xth Plenary Assembly," 30 Telecommunications Journal (ITU) 235 (Aug. 1963).

[12a] Since the submission of this article for publication the EARC was concluded successfully on November 8, 1963 with the signing of

The establishment of such a system, however, will also call for a high degree of international business cooperation. United States interests cannot alone construct, own and operate such a system. The United States is at only one end of each international message originating or terminating within its boundaries. Experience has shown that the other major nations, through their communications administrations or agencies, will wish to participate on a basis of equality. They will provide their own ground stations and will insist upon part ownership in the satellites themselves. Therefore, the United States interests must cooperate with these foreign interests at every step of the way, and there are many areas in which agreement must be reached. To suggest a few: What system should be adopted and how should it be designed? What will it cost and how will that cost be shared? Who will provide the hardware? What arrangements will be made for the coordination of its operation and use?

On their face these seem like difficult questions, especially since there will be a number of countries involved.[13] But it is unlikely that they will be as imposing as they seem. The importance of international communications is recognized throughout the world. The establishment and maintenance of facilities for such communications have historically been accomplished with a minimum of difficulty and with little

---

an international agreement by some 70 participating countries. The agreement, which is subject to ratification by the U.S. Senate, is scheduled to become effective January 1, 1965. The conference set aside 2800 megacycles for communications satellite service, 100 being allocated on an exclusive basis and 2700 shared with other services. The conditions under which sharing of the frequency bands is to be carried out were based on technical recommendations previously adopted by the CCIR. Although there are many footnotes and protocols indicating reservations by certain countries to specific allocations, the over-all result of the conference was highly satisfactory and provides a workable basis for development of worldwide satellite communication service.

[13] See, *e.g.*, Estep and Kearse, "Space Communications and the Law: Adequate International Control After 1963," 60 Mich. L. Rev. 873, 897-98 (May 1962).

regard to the temperature of the diplomatic climate short of war.[14] To illustrate, the American Telephone and Telegraph Company alone has operating agreements with communications agencies in 178 countries and areas, including the Iron Curtain countries and Cuba. Arrangements with Cuba have continued on a reasonably normal basis even under the Castro regime and despite its nationalization of Cuban communication interests and facilities.

One of the prime functions of the new Communications Satellite Corporation, which was incorporated on February 1, 1963, will be the solution of these questions through business negotiations with the communications administrations or agencies of the other interested countries. In the exercise of this function, the Communications Satellite Act provides that whenever the corporation enters into business negotiations with any international or foreign entity it shall notify the Department of State of the negotiations.[15] The Department of State shall thereupon advise the corporation of relevant foreign policy considerations concerning which the corporation must keep the Department of State informed throughout the negotiations. It is also specifically provided that, "The corporation may request the Department of State to assist in the negotiations, and that Department shall render such assistance as may be appropriate." [16]

There is ample precedent to which the corporation may turn for guidance in its negotiations.[17] The existing cable

[14] See Wingert, "New Tools for Global Communications," XLII Bell Tel. Mag. 2, 10 (Summer 1963).

[15] 76 Stat. 419, § 402, 47 U.S.C.A. § 742. In addition, the Act provides that the President shall supervise the relationship between the corporation and foreign governments and stimulate foreign participation in the system. See, e.g., § 201(a) (4) and (5).

[16] Ibid., § 402.

[17] The relative roles of the Federal Government and the Satellite Corporation are discussed at length in a reflective paper by Professor Estep, which was delivered at the Conference on the Law of Space and of Satellite Communications, May 2, 1963, at the Northwestern University School of Law, 58 N.W. U. L. Rev., 237 (1963).

and radio facilities can connect a telephone user in the United States with 98 per cent of the world's telephones and this includes more than 90 per cent of the telephones in Asia and Africa. A. T. & T. today has approximately 900 oversea telephone circuits in operation, of which about 600 are provided by modern submarine telephone cables which were placed in service starting in 1956, and the balance by high frequency or tropo-scatter radio. Cables, which provide both substantially greater capacity and superior quality of transmission, are being laid quite rapidly to meet the ever-increasing demand for improved international communications facilities. There are now three transatlantic cables, two to England and one to France, and cables to Alaska, Bermuda, Cuba, Hawaii, Jamaica, Panama and Puerto Rico. A cable to Japan via Hawaii and Guam is under construction and is scheduled to be completed by mid 1964. In addition, there are plans for another cable to France in mid 1965 and for further cables to Colombia via Jamaica and Panama, to St. Thomas, to Venezuela and to the Philippines. The British are also well along on the establishment of a Commonwealth Cable System which will link other widely separated areas throughout the world.

How have our cable and conventional radio facilities been established? In the case of radio the problem has been relatively simple. The communications agency at each end has agreed to establish its own transmitting and receiving facilities operating on a common frequency, and an agreement has been reached for the division of revenues derived from the service, generally on a 50-50 basis. Where, however, there are intermediate facilities required to provide service, such as undersea cables or satellites in outer space, provisions must be made for their construction, ownership and use. A brief explanation of the arrangements for the second transatlantic telephone cable (TAT 2) may be helpful in suggesting a possible pattern for the establishment of a communications satellite system.

TAT 2 was constructed under an agreement between the French Administration for Posts, Telegraphs and Telephones, the German Bundespost, and A. T. & T. Agreement was first reached as to the design of the cable, in this case the design being that of Bell Telephone Laboratories. It was also concluded that the cable should land at Penmarch, France, and that the French Administration would provide the German Bundespost with facilities across France. A. T. & T. was assigned the responsibility for constructing and laying the cable, and it was agreed that the cable would be paid for and owned, in common, in undivided shares by the three parties in the following ratios: The French Administration, 18.05 per cent, the German Administration, 18.05 per cent, and A. T. & T., 63.90 per cent. The cable initially was to have a capacity of 36 circuits and these circuits were allocated as follows: 13 circuits were assigned to A. T. & T. and the French Administration for U.S./France communications, 13 to A. T. & T. and the German Administration for U.S./German communications, and the remaining 10 circuits were assigned to A. T. & T. for communications between the United States and such other European countries as might wish to take an interest in the cable. It was also agreed that maintenance and operating costs would be paid by the parties in proportion to their ownership interests. By subsequent agreements with A. T. & T., Switzerland, Belgium, the Netherlands, Italy, and Spain have taken a one-half interest in one or more circuits assigned to A. T. & T. for the purpose, upon paying one-half of the capital costs allocable to such circuits and undertaking to pay in the future one-half of the maintenance and operating costs. In addition, circuits to France and Germany have been leased to certain United States international telegraph carriers.

This pattern, which has as its basic premise undivided common ownership of the communications capacity which is used to communicate between any two countries, recognizes the respective national interests of the countries involved and has been followed in all of A. T. & T.'s international cable agreements. It is flexible in that provision can be made for new countries to join in the use of the facilities either by capital contributions or by the leasing of circuits in the case of those who cannot afford to take an ownership interest. The adaptation of this pattern to a commercial framework for satellite communications should be given serious consideration.

While A. T. & T. was assigned the responsibility to construct and lay the TAT 2 cable, quite understandably, both the French and German Administrations desired that the manufacture of parts of the cable be done in their respective countries. Since in both countries there were manufacturers who were competent to manufacture the cable to A. T. & T.'s design, it was agreed that a manufacturer in each country should make a thousand miles of cable, excluding the submarine repeaters. Whether and to what extent the foreign administrations participating in the satellite system may similarly wish to provide hardware or services are questions for the future. While recent reports indicate that the foreign administrations are naturally anxious to provide equipment and services for the system,[18] few countries have rockets capable of putting communications satellites in orbit, and launching is where some of the largest costs will be incurred.

We in this country are well ahead in the technologies which can make international commercial satellite communi-

[18] "Postal and telegraph officials from 15 European countries met at Church House, London, last month to discuss how Europe can cooperate in American projects for a globestraddling satellite communications system. . . . They insist that if Europe goes along with American plans it should not be merely as a customer for an American-managed system. . . . The delegates reportedly agreed that Europe should contribute to a single satellite network, along with the U.S., since it would be irrational to have two or more rival space systems. However, the Europeans will demand much more scope in providing material, including the satellites themselves, and in running the show." McInnes, "Eldo to Esro," Barron's, Aug. 12, 1963, p. 5.

cations a reality within the next few years. It will nevertheless take high qualities of leadership to perfect the necessary commercial arrangements with the interested foreign administrations. We all hope and expect that the new satellite corporation will supply this leadership. In my judgment, however, these arrangements cannot be achieved through high level international conferences or conventions.[19]

The State Department's Richard Gardner has said that "No Congress of Vienna can promulgate a regime of law and order in outer space," and that "this objective will have to be developed through cooperative arrangements on specific functional problems."[20] In the case of communications satellites, we shall need to continue to make use of the good offices of the ITU to work out frequency assignments and to provide technical standards.[21] But satellite communications

---

[19] See, also, Feldman, "Communications Satellite Legislation and International Cooperation," 7 Antitrust Bull. 431, 436 (1962): "While these multilateral arrangements are not impossibilities, they may be more complicated approaches and fraught with more perils in negotiation and administration than a more cautious bilateral approach which is generally foreseen as the immediate pattern."

And, see, Schwartz and Goldsen, "Foreign Participation in Communications Satellite Systems," Rand Memorandum, RM-3484-RC, at 74 (Feb. 1963): "But it would be premature, and possibly injurious to the Act's objective of making the new service available as promptly as possible, to bring a great number of countries to the bargaining table at the outset."

[20] Gardner, "Cooperation in Outer Space," 41 Foreign Affairs 344, 359 (Jan. 1963).

[21] See Gross and Stead, "Telecommunication and Peaceful Uses of Outer Space," a paper submitted to UN Conference on the Application of Science and Technology for the Benefit of the Less Developed Areas, Agenda L.5.4 (Geneva, Jan. 1963).

Cf. the earlier statement of the then Under Secretary of State, George McGhee, before the Senate Aeronautical and Space Sciences Committee, 87th Cong., 2d Sess., at 162 (Feb. 28, 1962): "I would agree with Mr. Gross (Secretary General of the ITU) that the ITU is not suitable for conducting such an operation. If the ITU is to maintain its integrity as a regulatory and coordinating body for all media of international telecommunications, it cannot properly be made an operating agency. Its primary tasks in the international telecommunications field are those concerned with frequency allocation and other communication

should not become a pawn in a larger diplomatic game. This, must be a matter of business negotiations with the foreign communication administrations and agencies. They are in the communications business and are responsible for both the internal and external communications facilities and services of their respective countries. Their knowledge of, and interest in, communications is very great. Communications people talk a common language although they may not speak a common tongue. It is largely for these reasons that our existing international facilities have been established and maintained cooperatively and with a minimum of difficulty. There is every reason to believe that international satellite communications can be established and conducted in like manner. Recent discussions between representatives of the Satellite Corporation and a number of foreign administrations indicate that a good start has already been made in this direction.

It remains true that the totality of the task facing the new corporation is very large. Now that it is organized, its management must shortly arrange for an initial stock issue. Fifty per cent of this issue must be offered to private investors in "a manner to encourage the widest distribution to the American public." [22] The remaining 50 per cent will be reserved for communications common carriers authorized to

---

problems of international concern. It is the Department's view that it would be placing an undue burden on the International Telecommunications Union if it is to act as a regulatory and operating body at the same time."

See, also, Schwartz and Goldsen, *op. cit. supra*, n.19 at 78-79: "To turn over the development and establishment of the system to a supra-national agency at this time—whatever the political gains for one or another country—would undoubtedly delay the establishment of the system. Neither the ITU nor any other supra-national agency has the present authority or ability to operate this type of system, and the founders of a new agency for this purpose would face not only the negotiating problems described above, but many others as well."

[22] 76 Stat. 419, § 304(a), 47 U.S.C.A. § 734(a).

own stock in the new corporation by the Federal Communications Commission.[23]

Representations made to the public concerning the stock must be carefully framed. President Kennedy himself said that "There may be quite a long period of time before there is any return on this investment," and that he was "not sure the dollars and cents return would be comparable to what (investors) might be able to get in other areas, at least for a great many years."[24] There can be no basic disagreement with these statements. On the other hand, it will be material to disclose that the issuer is a corporation created by Congressional authority to carry out a national objective. The Incorporators are fully aware of their responsibilities, and in their first report to the President stated:

> "The initial stock offering, with the objective of widespread ownership by the general public, also presents unique challenges. The opportunity to participate in this venture will be given at a time when answers to some important questions will necessarily be incomplete. It will be our policy to obtain the best possible information on anticipated costs, cash flow, earnings, technical developments, and related matters, and to state the facts as we understand them, fully and frankly, to the American people."[25]

The corporation vigorously adhered to these views in an exchange of correspondence with the Federal Communications Commission. The Commission, in approving an authorization for an additional $600,000 under a line of credit established by the corporation, expressed concern over "the apparent lack of progress" in arrangements for the initial

---

[23] *Ibid.*, § 304(b).

[24] Statement of President Kennedy at his Press Conference on March 21, 1962, reported in the Wall Street Journal, March 22, 1962, at 1.

[25] Report on Activities and Accomplishments Under the Communications Satellite Act, Message from the President to Congress, H. Doc. No. 56, 88th Cong., 1st Sess., at 8 (Feb. 4, 1963).

offering of stock. Mr. Leo D. Welch, Chairman of the Board, responded:

"We urge that the members of the Commission recognize that to proceed with appropriate and essential studies in advance of the public offering of stock, as we have done and as we shall continue to do, does not show any lack of progress in arranging for a public offering. Rather it indicates sound preparation for an offering which when made will be consistent with the purposes and objectives of the Act and in which there will be provided to prospective investors a responsible presentation of material facts in compliance with the applicable federal and state securities laws. Such a program conforms with the views of the incorporators of the Corporation, as stated in their report to the President at the time of the organization of the Corporation:

" 'We recognize that the American people cannot be asked to support an enterprise of prime importance to the Nation and the world without sound knowledge of the public policy, technology, and economics that will govern it; of the people who will be responsible for its operations; of the relations with governments and with industry, at home and abroad, which will determine its viability; of the services it aspires to provide; of the nature and dimensions of the organization it plans to establish. We recognize at the same time that these questions should be resolved in ways that permit maximum flexibility in adapting to unpredictable developments in this uncharted field.'

"While firm answers to questions of this type will obviously not be forthcoming prior to the initial offering of stock, we believe that sufficient consideration must be given to provide the investor with an adequate basis for making a proper judgment. We propose to continue those studies required for a responsible presentation of material facts to the prospective investors as dictated by a sound regard for the establishment of a successful enterprise. We are hopeful that, consistently with such a program, we shall be in a position to approach the capital market not later than the early part of 1964." [26]

The economics of the enterprise, as Mr. Welch pointed out in his letter, "are highly sensitive to a large number of technical factors." Everyone seems to agree that ultimately the corporation should earn a profit but no one has categorically predicted when that will be.[27] Too many variables cloud the crystal ball. How much will the initial system cost? This will depend in part on the type of system and the extent of its coverage both in time and in territory. How long will the satellites last? One report has called satellite reliability the key technological problem.[28] When will the system become commercially operational? Until then there can be no revenues, but there will be expense. The best present estimates seem to be 1966 if all goes very well. Unforeseen technical difficulties, organizational delays, prolonged negotiations with foreign participants and other factors could postpone that date.

Once established, the usage of the system will have a controlling impact on the profit picture. It will be a high

---

[26] See 29 Telecommunications Rep. 1 (Aug. 12, 1963). On Aug. 14, 1963 in a speech to the Communications Committee of the American Bar Association, Mr. Henry, Chairman of the Commission stated: "I want to add that our recently publicized differences are more apparent than real, and I am confident that we are now in basic agreement."

[27] Reiger, Nichols, Early & Dews, "Communications Satellites: Technology, Economics and System Choices," Rand Memorandum, RM-3487-RC (Feb. 1963); Meckling, "The Economic Importance of Space Technology," Rand Memorandum, P-2585 (1962); Meckling, "Economic Potential of Communications Satellites," 133 Science 1885 (1961); Booz, Allen & Hamilton, "Telecommunication Satellite—Business Planning Study for Lockheed Aircraft Corp." (1960).

[28] Reiger, et al., *op. cit. supra*, n.27 at iii, 1, 5, 26-27.

capacity system, probably the equivalent of at least 1200 telephone circuits. This will substantially exceed the initial demand.[29] Charges which the corporation makes for satellite circuits will affect the demand, both as they relate to the cost of circuits in alternative facilities, such as cables, and to the rates charged by the carriers to the public for service. In this connection it is important to understand that no one seriously advocates that satellites should replace submarine cables. Reliable and secure international communications require both. The cable art has advanced rapidly since the first transatlantic telephone cable was placed in service in 1956 and within the next few years there will be high capacity transistorized cables capable of providing more than 700 circuits.

The new corporation will be a common carrier's common carrier fully subject to regulation by the Federal Communications Commission. Challenging regulatory questions will arise.[30] The corporation will, of necessity, live off its capital until at least a part of the system is in operation and revenue producing. What accounting and rate-making treatment will be accorded the losses it will incur until its income meets its outgo? Will its charges for leasing circuits to the United States international communications common carriers be fixed so as to maximize earnings at the earliest possible time and, if so, how? The ultimate source of revenues to support the investment in the corporation will be the monies received by the United States carriers for service to the public via the satellite system. How will the charges of the United States carriers to the public for services originating in the United

---

[29] Reiger, et al., *op. cit. supra*, n.27 at iii: "The key economic problem is that of demand, for the minimum costs of a satellite system will be large, and the circuit capacities provided will represent a large increment over existing capacities." See also 57-71.

[30] See Strassburg, "Space Communications—A New Chapter in Regulation," Ann. Rep., Sec. of Pub. Util. Law, Amer. Bar Ass'n, 23, 31-36 (1963).

States be harmonized with the like charges by the foreign administrations for services in the reverse direction?

These and a host of other problems attend the undertaking. They are far from insoluble, but their solution will require a very high degree of business, scientific and regulatory understanding and talent.

5

Richard A. Falk

TOWARD A RESPONSIBLE PROCEDURE FOR THE NATIONAL ASSERTION OF PROTESTED CLAIMS TO USE SPACE

Controversial claims about the use of outer space raise issues of utmost importance for the future of world order. There are two principal explanations of this importance. First, the regulation of space is itself a substantive matter of major concern. Second, the problems of space regulation illustrate the pervasive difficulty in world affairs of restraining new behavior by powerful states. In the course of this essay, we shall concentrate upon this more general question.

The loosely structured character of international society accounts for part of the explanation why novel claims are troublesome. There is no regularly available legislature or executive to adapt the regulative framework to new and unanticipated areas of human development. If the actors, who assert new claims that are of consequence not just to themselves but to the entire community, are powerful states, then international society seems particularly unequipped, formally or actually, to insist that community interests be given precedence over national interests. The ideology and the realism of the doctrine of national sovereignty make powerful nations rather unamenable to restraint imposed, so to speak, from above. This is precisely the situation in the space field. Powerful nations are developing a new technology that is already having, and will increasingly possess, a global significance. Yet these nations are acting in almost exclusive response to the dictates of their national will. What is more pertinent is that whatever community will exists will lack the capability to express itself effectively. Such a situation lies in the background of the excitement that surrounds the opening of the space age.

If we acknowledge the primacy of the sovereign actor in the space field, then it is necessary to examine the prospects for a sovereign willingness to substitute regulation for anarchy. Perhaps the tradition of legal positivism gives grounds for hope. By asserting that valid international obligations can arise only as a result of the consent of the sovereign to be bound, it may appear possible to entice the space powers to generate their own regulatory scheme by drawing up a comprehensive space code. For the space powers are not cut off from the interests that prompt the community of states to seek a regime of restraint and a safeguarding of the supranational interests at stake. There is a mix of national interests that supplements the traditional drive to preserve a maximum area of sovereign discretion with an equally traditional drive to substitute mutual restraint for unregulated competition. This drive for order is certainly present, even if it is not yet dominant, in the space area. For it is widely appreciated that it would be desirable to avoid the extension of the arms race between the Soviet Union and the United States to activities in outer space. Such military competition would be expensive and dangerous. The weapons are difficult to develop and it is hard to monitor the progress of one's rival(s). Some evidence of restraint is present.

At the same time, certain uses of space with military significance have been already undertaken. There has been no effort to prohibit the passage of guided missiles through outer space. The fact of space passage has not been regarded as a significant differentiating variable in discussions about the legality of missiles or nuclear weapons. Then, too, the collection by space satellites of information with military significance has been evidently undertaken, but not without arousing strong Soviet protest. These protests have emphasized the argument that a state should not be able to use space to gather information that it is not able to obtain legally by other means. Decisions about military uses of space have been made by sovereign states largely as a consequence of procedures internal to government, the substantive workings of which are not fully disclosed to the public. This is especially true for the Soviet Union, but it is also apparent that the government of the United States has not revealed fully the military uses that it now makes and proposes in the future to make of outer space.

To examine the nature of the problem, I would like to consider the Samos-Midas observation satellite program as a hypothetical instance of a potential military use of space. The justification for Samos-Midas as a particular policy cannot be appraised. An appraisal depends, in part at least, upon elaborate security arguments in favor of information-gathering. These arguments cannot be evaluated without access to highly classified materials, for instance, the availability of alternate information sources, the success of satellite missions, the relation of this information to such matters as protection against surprise attack, the over-building and under-building of a deterrent force, and the development of a credible first and second strike posture. The military argument also requires a reliance upon unavailable estimates about Soviet capabilities, vulnerabilities, and intentions vis-à-vis nuclear war. Thus it is not possible to come to a prudent substantive conclusion about the advisibility of the Samos-Midas program. What is possible, however, is to discuss considerations that are relevant to the formation of national policy with respect to a military use of space that has generated protests on the part of another dominant space power. Inquiry will concern the development of procedures to assure the adoption of a reasonable course of action, appraising "reasonable" from the dual perspective of national and global interests. A basic assumption is made that a powerful state in the contemporary world should act to improve world order as well as to promote sovereign advantage.

An adequate understanding of this kind of problem rests upon the character of law and order in world affairs today. Part of an improved approach involves the adoption of a clearer policy toward the mix between national and community will on various issues. There is no abstract formula that will instruct states on the extent of deference to be accorded to formal expressions of consensus by the majority of states. Each substantive area presents distinct considerations about the scope of sovereign discretion. This kind of balancing analysis, common for federal states required to reconcile the powers of the central government with those of its members states, is rather new for international affairs. It is also very different. For unlike the characteristic federal state, there remains no disposition to move preponderant power and authority to the political center of international society. The national units in the international system, especially the space users, retain predominant power and competence. Given these facts of political dispersal, what is the extent of and the basis for the effective curtailment of national power? This is the most appropriate starting-point for any meditation upon the foundations of world legal order.

It is an especially attractive point of origin for thinking about the legal regulation, if any, of contested uses of outer space. For there is no background of use to provide a tradition of restraint. These are new claims to act in a realm of activity that was previously non-existent. It is possible, although not very convincing, to analogize outer space to air space or to maritime regions. This provides, by analogy, a tradition of restraint, but there are so many significant differences and the analogous standards are so vague that what points of contact exist can be manipulated at whim.

Another way to raise the issue is to question the postulate of legal positivism that sovereign consent, presumed or express, must underlie every valid international obligation. Perhaps the United Nations can restrain space claims that are detrimental to world community welfare. But practice indicates that the General Assembly does not possess the kind of legislative competence that will be respected, especially when exercised to control vital activities undertaken by major states. For instance, the appeals by the United Nations in the areas of nuclear testing and disarmament, although perhaps responsible for continuing disarmament discussions, suggest the rather modest extent of United Nations effectiveness. Certainly norms posited by the Organization, but not perceived as serving the common interests of the space nations, are not likely to constrain conduct, unless they are formulated on very abstract levels and tolerate the unreliability of self-interpretation. There are no central institutions in international society that possess the strength to impose their will upon dissenting powerful states.

This absence of centralized effective authority is a critical fact of international life. If the organized community cannot impose restraint, then restraint, if it is to exist at all, must be self-generated. An obvious inference is that the parties to be restrained must come to an agreement, *i.e.*, that in this case the space powers must enter into a compact of mutual restraint that satisfies their joint and separate interests. But, as the disarmament negotiations suggest, to advocate this end is not to disclose a way to reach it. Lack of trust, asymmetrical strategic space objectives, absence of a domestic consensus, unwillingness to give up sovereign prerogatives, and uncertainty about what will be uncovered by subsequent space development all contribute to a climate of opinion that remains hostile to a search for a code of space law and administration at this time. Perhaps either limited agreements of importance can be reached as, for example, to prohibit the orbiting of weapons, or broad agreements of useless generality can be achieved. It is clear, however, that no general regime of space restraint can be presently negotiated by the parties, nor can it be effectively imposed by the organized community of states.

But do these discouraging conclusions warrant an acceptance of anarchy plus national egoism in the use of space? This would be the traditionalist response to the absence of a prospect for formal order. This essay urges a more constructive response, partly as a policy argument about how the United States should act and partly as an illustration of lawmaking in a horizontal (a relatively unstructured) social system. The basic argument is that a nation should adopt what amounts to the golden rule as a guide to its action and should refrain from making the kind of claim that it would not want to be made against it. Such an adherence to the ground rules of reciprocity is posited as an aspect of minimum world order in the nuclear age. But suppose this attitude of self-restraint is itself unreciprocated? Suppose our space rivals pursue an egocentric policy that is restrained only by the vagaries of their dubious prudence and the exertions of their growing capability? Shall we cripple ourselves in the competitive struggle for strategic superiority in a world of conflict and hostility? The security considerations raised by these questions cannot and should not be avoided altogether. For this reason it is necessary in a specific case to assess the costs of unilateral restraint. Thus one must refrain from reaching substantive conclusions on such a question as whether the United States should go ahead with a space observation system in the face of Soviet protest.

But it is also important to affirm that the golden rule approach has not been tested in the space area or, for that matter, in any other area of developing national power. For this reason it is important to make explicit the reasons why a nation acts or refrains from acting in the face of protest. Only then can it be fairly seen whether or not Soviet patterns will evolve to incorporate a golden rule approach into their peaceful co-existence framework for international affairs.

We are also concerned with the legality of claims arising out of a subject that exists within a normative vacuum. Where there are no pre-existing rules and no persuasive analogies, is everything permitted? Our examination of the legality of observation satellites tries to develop the basis for a partial negative answer. It is partial because it asserts a procedure for making novel claims, but it lacks any substantive rules to identify an impermissible claim. The main elements in the procedure are easily summarized. First, there is an obligation to disclose to the extent possible the justification for asserting the claim in the face of protest (an unprotested national claim is permissible, if its nature is disclosed, at this stage in international law). Second, the argument opposing the claim must be fairly considered, including any detrimental effects on the future of world order. And, third, the sentiments of the community, especially as formally expressed through the United Nations should be taken into account. Of course, this procedure is not very directive in a specific case. A claim resting upon an undisclosed military justification cannot be fully assessed. But the destabilizing effect of asserting a claim that is arbitrary on the basis of what can be disclosed is apparent and should be an inhibiting feature of its assertion for a responsible actor. Of course, advocacy of the golden rule is only a plea for the acceptance of a primitive species of legal order. But a rudimentary system of legal restraint is better than none at all. Our present choice seems to be primarily between the improvement of the claiming procedures of space states and the acceptance of a dangerous anarchy. It is true that some opportunities for formal agreement on specific issues moderate the sharpness of the choice. The constructive task, then, is to examine the extent to which the development of more responsible national procedures for asserting space claims over protest adds to these opportunities to moderate activity by formal international agreement.

The strategic importance of observational intelligence to the Cold War presently makes this subject-matter an intractable area for isolated international negotiation. We have seen increasingly that neither the Soviet Union nor the United

States is likely to forgo strategic advantages in the Cold War in order to promote the cause of world order. We need only refer to the 1961 Soviet resumption of nuclear testing or to the 1956 Hungarian intervention or to the initiation of nuclear testing by the United States on the high seas or to our participation in the armed invasion of Cuba in April 1961 in order to sense the Cold War pressure to overcome considerations favoring restraint. Viewed in this light, the prospects are indeed slim for depoliticizing a controversy about the status of observation from outer space.

We can summarize the extra-legal conditioning of the observational satellite program, then, by reviewing the opposed military strategies and contradictory interpretations of motive on the part of the Cold War rivals. The USSR regards reconnaissance from outer space as a threat to its survival since it tends to locate targets for a thermonuclear surprise attack and to impair the tradition (with Czarist credentials) of secrecy about military affairs. The United States, in contrast, links its survival to an adequate warning system that will stabilize deterrence and discourage surprise attack.

How is such a conflict to be resolved? Is it a discretionary right of the United States to orbit reconnaisance satellites over the Soviet Union? And, is it a discretionary right of the Soviet Union to shoot them down if it can? Have we no way, other than by force, to vindicate or refute such a claim on the frontier of technological development in outer space? How do we attain limits for national conduct in an area where there is neither authoritative practice nor converging interests to support an agreement? We require a technique of evaluation that enlarges the horizon of relevance beyond the confines of military strategy.

How shall we characterize the activity of the observational satellite program? Is it "espionage"? Does it matter? Traditional definitions of espionage emphasize its *clandestine character*, and thus it can be argued that the "openness" of satellite intelligence activity puts it outside the scope of espionage.[1] This attitude might view the satellite program as a unilateral attempt to do what the Open Skies proposal sought on a bilateral basis. This interpretation would, however, be more persuasive if the United States had come forward with a proposal for the internationalization of the activity under United Nations control.[2] Observation from outer space would then become assimilated into the special needs for the maintenance of peace in a nuclear age.[3] This claim deserves special consideration and requires a careful differentiation of the *potential* role of this activity from the egoistic, secret use of traditional espionage.

Such an interpretative problem underlies the Soviet claims that outer space is only available for non-military uses (except in the event of war) and that the observational intelligence program is a military use—since it is financed and administered by the United States armed forces and thus related to the military effort. The precedent of claiming the right to use outer space for peace-time military purposes is a very dangerous one. We must keep in mind the relevance of reciprocity and estoppel in an area of behavior that lacks clear legal norms. For example, use of outer space by A

---

[1] Crane's "Planning for Space Legal Policy" (a paper presented to the American Rocket Society, October 1961) develops a similar position in explicating what he calls the "motivation for space policy;" for instance, he says "(t)he basic thesis of this paper is that law is gaining increasing value as an instrument to deny control of outer space to others, and that the potential advantage of a law-oriented space policy should be integrated into military contingency planning." Contrast this approach with that taken in "Aerospace Force in the Sixties," symposium in 12 *Air University Quarterly Review* 1 (Winter and Spring 1960-61).

[2] *E.g.* consider definition given in the "Espionage" article in the *Encyclopedia of the Social Sciences*, V, 594 (1931); "Espionage is the practice of obtaining information about an actual or potential enemy clandestinely for possible use against the enemy."

[3] Quigg, "Open Skies and Open Space," Legal Problems of Space Exploration, prepared for Senate Committee on Astronautical and Space Sciences, Doc. No. 26, 87th Cong., 1st Sess. (1961), *Legal Problems* 463; Young, "The Aerial Inspection Plan and Air Space Sovereignty," *Id.* at 46.

warrants an equivalent [4] use by B and diminishes the prospect for an effective objection by A. Thus, A's use establishes a permissive norm. This basic pattern of international law-making should encourage sober reflection before unilateral claims are asserted at the frontiers of military technique. For instance, in looking back on nuclear testing, we wonder whether the United States would not have helped its cause *on every level* by pressing for a test ban or a limitation in advance rather than by following a unilateral pattern of claim, subsequent estoppel, and eventual anxious dismay.

There are various ways to approach a legal analysis of space surveillance. For instance, one might emphasize the fact the satellites gather and transmit their information without entering the target state.[5] This means that there is no interference with the administration of the national society. For example, the efforts to recruit and catch spies are objectionable aspects of espionage activities. Observation from outer space by unmanned satellites, on the other hand, does not inject an information-gathering foreign agent into the life blood of the social order. It has been suggested that there is an analogy between the space observation program and the permissible photographic observation of shore objects from aircraft overflying the high seas.[6] However, this legitimation is qualified by the general duty to use the high seas in a manner that does not infringe upon the rights of the shore state and, further, by the evident right of the observed state to view such observation as "aggressive" or "military"

---

[4] Equivalent use does not mean identical use; thus, a military use of outer space by A that serves its strategic needs makes a proportionate use by B legitimate, given its peculiar strategic needs. *Cf.* a rather attenuated suggestion of equivalence between Sputnik and U-2 overflights by Lipson, "The Gagarin and Powers Flights," 17 *Bulletin of the Atomic Scientists* 274 (1961).

[5] This formulation implicitly assumes that the Samos-Midas satellites operate in "outer space" and that outer space is outside of national territory.

[6] See Cooper, "Letter to the Editor," *Spaceflight*, III, No. 2, 99 (1961).

and to take appropriate protective measures.[7] This description of "the law" informs us only about the rhetorical techniques used by participants in a decentralized legal order faced with a conflict between claim (US observation) and objection (Soviet retaliation). As will be shown, the international legal order possesses techniques for a decentralized appraisal of legality that applies to the surveillance controversy. It has been generally conceded that a nation can forbid others to photograph strategic objects and events taking place within its territory. All nations, including the United States and the Soviet Union, strictly regulate and punish land-based activity that seeks to obtain the information that satellites are able to collect from outer space. The Chicago Convention on International Civil Aviation, many instances of uncontested national legislation, and the 1960 U-2 incident in the Soviet Union all convincingly extend this power of prohibition to unauthorized information-gathering that is conducted in territorial air-space. It seems generally agreed that unauthorized information and photographing fall within the developing concept of "espionage." In fact, even our newspapers have dubbed observation satellites as "space spies," "spy in the sky," and the like. State practice and general usage both argue for the treatment of unauthorized aerial observation as "espionage" that is subject to regulation by the victim state.

It is plausible to stress the extra-territorial character of space surveillance. This permits us to emphasize the territorial limits of national sovereignty and the non-territorial status of outer space. For the state that is the target of observation, however, it matters little where the observer locates himself. The functional quality of espionage from outer space is, at least from the viewpoint of the information gathered, no different from espionage in airspace. Deputy Attorney General Katzenbach has perhaps overstated this point when he suggested that the height of the activity is of no relevance to a

---

[7] *Id.* at 100.

proper determination of its validity.[8] Certainly, the trend is toward the replacement of mechanical criteria by contextual judgments that rely upon a functional analysis as the basis for the proper delimitation of jurisdictional competence. Rather than relying upon the physical locus of constituent acts or upon some other isolated qualifying element of the facts (for instance, the nationality of the actor), it is thought preferable to urge a comprehensive appraisal of the reasonableness of the particular claim by a reference to all affected interests.[9] A jurisdictional decision, then, would depend upon a balancing of the competing interests of claimant and protesting states. This jurisdictional model of decision-making is primarily applicable to the practice of national courts, but it is also useful here, where executive officials of the United States are called upon to decide whether to make a unilateral claim. The process of rational decision, as McDougal has shown so well, is structurally similar, regardless of where the decision-maker is located in the social process.[10]

It seems reasonable for a state to characterize surveillance from outer space as "espionage." This puts it easily within the legislative reach of Soviet law. For it is legitimate to prosecute for espionage even if the defendant acts in foreign territory. The reach of United States economic regulation serves to illustrate this kind of a claim in a situation in which the prosecuting state has a less direct and acknowledged in-

---

[8] Katzenbach, "Law and Lawyers in Space," 14 *Bulletin of the Atomic Scientists*, 221, 222: "Whether it (a satellite) is higher or lower is irrelevant to the objections an observer state would posit or the claims the observer would make."

[9] Falk, "Juisdiction, Immunities, and Act of State: Suggestions for a Modified Appoach," in *Essays on International Jurisdiction* (1961); Trautman, "The Role of Conflicts Thinking in Defining the International Reach of American Regulatory Legislation," 20 *Ohio State Law Journal* 586 (1961).

[10] See especially McDougal, "International Law, Power and Policy: A Contemporary Conception," 82 *Hague Recueil* 137 (1953).

terest;[11] that is, the extension of claims to protect national security has priority over claims to defend the economy. If a state can regulate espionage taking place in another sovereign state, then it certainly can impose equivalent regulation upon similar activity in outer space. Giving a status of "espionage" to the activity makes the locus of conduct irrelevant to the legislative claim. It seems clear, then, that the Soviet Union has the legislative competence to characterize the observation program as "espionage" and to prescribe appropriate remedies.

One of the most characteristic features of the international legal order is the wide discretion of nations to characterize activity for the purposes of applying their legal policy. The *Nottebohm* case illustrates the attempt of a supranational tribunal to discover limits to this power. It is enormously significant as a challenge to the tradition of decentralization. The extension of *Nottebohm* thinking is reflected in the "genuine link" requirement for merchant shipping that has found its way into the Geneva Convention on the Law of the High Seas as a rebuff to "flags of convenience." [12] Without vertical institutional development, however, it remains to be seen whether international order loses or gains by attempts to centralize and objectify the power to characterize. We give up the simple criterion of national discretion and yet provide no substitute with which to specify legal status. Is this not, then, a premature attempt to verticalize international legal order? Despite *Nottebohm*, it seems accurate to affirm the

---

[11] For instance, the controversial extraterritorial antitrust decisions: *United States* v. *Timken Roller Bearing Co.*, 341 U.S. 593 (1951); *United States* v. *Aluminum Co. of America*, 148 F. 2d 416, 443 (2d Cir. 1946); see generally U.S. *Attorney General's National Committee to Study the Antitrust Law Report* 66-91 (1955).

[12] Geneva Convention on the High Seas, UN Doc. A/CONF. 13/L. 53 and corr. 1 (1958) Article 5 (1): "Each State shall fix the conditions for the grant of its nationality to ships. . . . There must exist a genuine link between the State and the ship; in particular, the State must effectively exercise its jurisdiction and control in administrative, technical and social matters over ships flying its flag."

capacity of nations to characterize an activity that is a threat to its military security.[13] The United States claim of Air Defense Identification Zones appears to be a parallel instance.

However, for the surveillance program, and this is the novelty of the situation, the United States supports its claim by a reference to its military security. That is, we claim that the surveillance of the Soviet Union by our satellites is an essential precaution against surprise attack. The claim, in effect, makes espionage from outer space a matter of self-defense. Thus, in a formal sense, two irreconcilable claims are present. In a centralized system, this would call for the intervention of judicial or legislative action to resolve the competing claims by compromise or choice. But what is to be done in a relatively decentralized legal order?

The probable course of conduct in a decentralized legal order will be an exhibition of the maximum assertion of opposed national claims at each stage of the controversy. Thus, the United States will try to orbit the satellites, and the Soviet Union will try to shoot them down. However, a preferred course of conduct would question the reasonableness of the assertion of the claim, given competing interests, and make every effort to justify it to the target state. This applies more to the United States decision to orbit satellites than to the derivative Soviet decision to interfere with them. The nation that disturbs the *status quo ante* in a decentralized legal order bears the main burden for the ensuing instability.

The position of the United States, as the leader of the bloc resisting the expansion of the revolutionary nations, creates a special national interest in strengthening international order. It is not that we must sacrifice national security in order to

---

[13] This does, however, relieve the claimant state of the duty to use a rational process of self-delimitation when it proposes to extend its competence by unilateral action; reciprocity and estoppel operate to limit the unilaterabity of the process. See generally Falk, "International Jurisdiction: Horizontal and Vertical Conceptions of Legal Order," 32 *Temple Law Quarterly* 295 (1959).

promote world order but rather that we should see whether the sacrifice in world order is worth the gain in security. The U-2 incident, the sponsorship of the Cuban invasion of April 1961, the Connally Reservation, and the fight to keep Formosa on the Security Council all illustrate instances in which an overly narrow interpretation of national interests seems to impair the quality of contemporary world order without adequate justification. Likewise, there is no evidence that the decision to put the surveillance program into operation takes adequate account of its probable destabilizing effect on other activity in outer space. Thus far, outer space has been used compatibly by Cold War rivals for peaceful purposes. It seems hazardous to transfer the continuing uses of outer space into a Cold War arena. It is difficult, without access to intelligence appraisals, to suggest the probable net gain or loss from space observation. Nevertheless, it remains possible to urge a basis of decision that considers the consequences for world legal order, as well as the gains for military intelligence.

Espionage possesses the peculiar quality of being tolerated while it is, at the same time, treated as illegal.[14] This odd status, much like that of prostitution in many European countries, encourages a practice whereby states engage in espionage but do not come forward to defend an agent who is caught by enforcement techniques. Consider, for example,

---

[14] For the qualified assertion that "espionage of itself does not appear to constitute a violation of international law," see Note, "Legal Aspects of Reconnaissance in Airspace and Outer Space," 61 *Columbia Law Review* 1074 (1961) (see especially note 1 at p. 1074). Authoritive doctrine seems to be available to support such a conclusion, as well as considerable persuasive policy available to oppose it. An adequate analysis of the issue of "legality" would have to distinguish between information-gathering and the various kinds of subversion. Espionage is increasingly a part of the pattern of coercion roughly identified as "indirect aggression." The attempt to make the issue of legality rest upon the fact of war or peace seems to oversimplify the issue. For excellent discussion of wartime espionage (and the like), see Baxter, "So-Called 'Unprivileged Belligerency': Spies, Guerillas, and Saboteurs," 28 *British Yearbook of International Law* 323 (1951).

the Soviet forebearance from comment during the long trial of Colonel Abel together with the recent Soviet willingness to exchange Powers and Prior for Abel. The silence of the state sending the agent usually leads sanctions to be imposed *only* upon the detected agent, not his country. The employing state is not drawn formally into the espionage trial, nor is there any effort to insist upon the legal responsibility of the state that commissioned the espionage.

The space observation program, unless it can be kept secret, raises the same problems that proved so troublesome in the U-2 incident. This observation would seem to constitute "espionage" under *explicit* government auspices. Part of its legal quality would depend upon American motivation, especially the extent to which this information contributes to defensive rather than aggressive policies of national defense. In other words, the test for the relative illegality of espionage rests to some degree upon a judgment of the end being sought. However, in view of the usefulness of the satellites for aggressive purposes, this test would appear to impose a burden of demonstration upon the United States. The program is an attempt to undermine the security regulations of a sovereign state during peace-time and, as such, would seem to violate the independence of the target state. A strong argument could be made on behalf of the Soviet objections to an impartial decision-maker. The United Nations Security Council would be an appropriate forum for discussion and appraisal. Characteristically, as we have said, the government sponsoring "espionage" is not explicitly connected with its agents, and the enforcement state proceeds against the agent as an ordinary criminal defendant. But the satellite program presents a novel pattern of espionage activity that renders obsolete many of the enforcement concepts that were developed in the course of dealing with traditional espionage.

Presumably, the satellites, as governmental property devoted to a public use, would be entitled to sovereign immunity by application of normal principles. However, the use of satellites to break the laws of target states would, at least after warning, allow coercive action to be taken in self-protection. Furthermore, immunity is primarily a judicial inhibition. In any event, it is unlikely that the disposition of the controversy will stress to any degree the sovereign ownership of the satellites.

Finally, there is the Soviet claim to engage in extra-territorial enforcement. If we grant that outer space is "outside" of national territory, it is still quite tenable to reason, by analogy to the practice in contiguous zones on the high seas, that a state may make those claims that are reasonably necessary for its national security. Thus, there would be no need to claim sovereignty up to the heavens in order to justify Soviet enforcement of its espionage laws in outer space. The USSR could quite reasonably assert a particularized claim to control espionage, even if the objectionable acts were all performed in outer space. In jurisdictional rhetoric, it can be said that a jurisdictional claim to assert control over a particular activity in outer space does not rest upon the prior establishment of national sovereignty over outer space. Neither the physical locus of conduct nor sovereignty is an indispensable basis for valid jurisdictional claims. On the contrary, it is important to encourage the formulation of particularized claims, defended by their reasonable link to national interest, in preference to wholesale extensions of sovereignty that will validate, among other things, the particular claim.

The experience with territorial waters is instructive. Latin American claims to wide belts (200 to 300 miles) of territorial waters were primarily prompted by a desire to keep foreign trawling fleets out of coastal fisheries. It would have served this interest and kept a maximum area for free, unimpeded use of the high seas, had these nations instead put their claim in the kind of specific language used to justify national control *beyond* territorial waters.[15] The particular claim, justified by

---

[15] See Kaplan and Katzenbach, *The Political Foundations of International Law* 147-54 (1961); see also, McDougal and Burke, "Crisis in

reference to national interests, commends itself to the needs
of world order far more than does the crude exclusivity of the
notion of sovereignty. For, wherever it is functionally advantageous to share use, then it is best to work out a solution along
specific lines. The dichotomy between freedom (of high seas,
of outer space) and sovereignty is an inept way to allocate
legal competence in an area where most uses are inclusive but
a few are exclusive.[16] World order advances by accommodat-
ing these two sets of national interests: that is, by encouraging,
an awareness that national interests often profit more by for-
going exclusivity than by insisting upon it. The growth of
supranationalism in Europe, the Antarctic Treaty, and the
success of the specialized agencies of the United Nations bear
witness to an emerging realization that sovereignty is not the
answer to the allocation of authority and of resources with
respect to a subject-matter that is of genuine interest to more
than one nation. But such an auspicious development depends
upon the willingness of nations to refrain from using the
community forum as a base for hostile operations against a
member of the community. Here again, we sense the potential
harm that may be done by space observation. In the struggle
to minimize exclusive claims in outer space, it is dangerous to
jeopardize the perceived safety of other nations. For this
causes both the minimum basis for trust to disappear and the
functional compatibility of interests to vanish.

This discussion raises a general theoretical issue relevant
to the future course of international legal development. The
facts of progressive interdependence, frequently acknowledged
in recent literature, lead to a need for sharper allocational
concepts in the international legal system. When nations were
relatively independent in the pursuit of their interests, it was
desirable to stress the simplicity of the ideas of sovereign ex-

---

the Law of the Sea: Community Perspectives versus National Egoism," in
Studies in World Public Order, 844-911 (1960).

[16] The distinction between exclusive and inclusive is borrowed from
McDougal and Burke.

clusivity and inclusive freedom. Interdependence requires more subtle categories of international law in order to give maximum support to as many genuine national interests as possible. The encouragement of *ad hoc* justification for particular claims accords with this need. It allows the process of claim and of subsequent resistance to emphasize relative functional considerations rather than abstract categories of legal status. This seems to be the best way for an interdependent but decentralized legal order to ask whether it can solicit maximum support from national actors. This is very important, since the slow growth of supranational legal order depends heavily on the development of trust on the national level. And trust only emerges from the perception of a non-arbitrary attempt to serve the relevant community and its members.

This is related to the attempts of some commentators to solve the problems of outer space by using a rough analogy to the status of the airspace, the high seas, or the polar regions.[17] The historical process of claim underneath the crude doctrinal categories provides considerable guidance, especially with regard to the administration of the high seas. Professor Lipson has made this point with admirable succinctness:

> In maritime law and practice there is not merely a zone of territorial waters, a single contiguous zone, and the free high seas; there is a whole cluster of zones, overlapping and intersecting, established at different times for different purposes by different states (unilaterally, bilaterally, and multilaterally) with different degrees of formality, enforced by different methods, and accepted in different degrees by varying numbers of other states.

[17] Note, "National Sovereignty of Outer Space," 74 *Harvard Law Review* 1154, 1159-67 (1961); Lipson and Katzenbach, *Report to the National Aeronautics and Space Administration on the Law of Outer Space*, 77-83 (1960); Jessup and Taubenfeld, *Controls for Outer Space*, 160-90 (1959).

This general view is made quite concrete:

> No unitary rule could or should be devised to cover this motley patchwork; there is no reason why one rule of law must apply to the regulation, control, prohibition, or mutual tolerance of such diverse activities as navigation, fishing, conservation of fisheries, and cable-laying; naval maneuvers and antisubmarine patrol; the use and conservation of resources on the sea bed; enforcement of customs regulation; and protection of neutrality. *It is this very diversity of legal order, stemming from the diversity of policies and purposes, fitting the diversity of activities and conditions, that will provide a fruitful analogy for what must be a gradual development of the law of outer space.*[18]

This sophisticated approach to the use of analogy, stressing concrete legal problems rather than overarching doctrinal abstractions, is the basis for rational law-planning in outer space. The facts of interdependence, highlighted by the problem of distinguishing military and peaceful uses, make it essential that nations assert their claims with a clear sense of community welfare in mind. Allocations on the high seas could allow specific unilateral assertions based on a narrow view of national interest without often risking, until very recently, community welfare. Rational allocation of authority to act in outer space, however, requires a broader view of national interest that incorporates the genuine concerns of other nations, if it is to foster the growth of a legal regime based upon maximum use and minimum friction. It is with this emphasis that we urge an appraisal of the legality of the Samos-Midas program.

Does it matter that the observation satellites are unmanned? Such an inquiry is independent from, although related to, the earlier discussion of jurisdiction. It looks upon the issue from the special perspective of national sovereignty

---

[18] Both excerpts are from Lipson, *Outer Space and International Law* 10 (Rand Paper P-1434, 1958). Emphasis added.

and its distinctive ordering role in international affairs. Does a surface state have any sovereign control over the activity that takes place in "outer space"? President Kennedy has told the General Assembly of the United Nations that "[t]he new horizons of outer space must not be riven by the old bitter concepts of imperialism and sovereignty." [19] This presumably means that the development of outer space should not proceed by states claiming exclusive control over specified uses or regions of outer space. It looks toward some cooperative regime established and operated by legal institutions and techniques. However, "sovereignty" also refers to the capacity of states to generate legal order. But how can we overcome the contradictory national policies of Cold War rivals? With the objective of legal order in view, let us examine the ways in which disputes over contested uses of outer space might be handled under circumstances of present political conflict. Here, the role of national sovereignty—not as a way to validate claims to exclusive control but as an agent to establish the legitimacy of particular claims or to create a legal regime—is indeed complex.

We step into a dense jurisprudential jungle at this point. The delimitation of national sovereignty, as an ordering agency, is among the most slippery subjects in international law. It is especially problematic in a case such as this, where prior experience offers relatively little guidance. The legal order tends to resolve present controversies by referring to past norms and dispositions. When the past does not provide guidance and when the issue is important, the legal order in a centralized social system tends to generate a new solution by legislation. The international legal order lacks central legislative institutions; it depends, instead, upon decentralized ordering techniques to meet the challenge of a new situation. But the outer limit of innovation in a decentralized system is reached at the point where the interests of the powerful actors

---

[19] N. Y. *Times*, September 26, 1961.

within the system begin to diverge significantly. For international law, this means, among other things, that the equivalent of legislation—at least of a formal variety—must satisfy the dominant interests of powerful national actors. Thus, it is difficult to anticipate a formal resolution of a dispute, which is not covered by the inherited system,[20] when antagonistic interests of the United States and the Soviet Union arise from Cold War subject-matter.

This analysis seems suggestive for our attempt to understand the bearing of international law upon proposed uses by the United States of outer space for "espionage" against the Soviet Union. Those analysts who would resolve such a controversy by negotiating an agreement on the degree of national sovereignty over outer space seem to overlook the relevance of the character of the international system to the prescription of new norms. The incapacity of the international system to provide orderly ways to test new claims is a serious cause of contemporary instability. A nation is given the choice of self-restraint or of recourse to unilateral action backed by force. The danger of shifting a choice back onto the national level is illustrated by Israel's initiation of the Suez campaign in 1956 and by the revolts of oppressed peoples in Africa. The Samos-Midas program also illustrates the inflexibility of the system. There is no institutionalized way to determine the validity of the United States claim, and the two nuclear bloc leaders must settle the issue by give and take, since neither United States

---

[20] The reference here is to the problem of adjusting the international legal system—a development of Western European culture—to a plurality of contemporary normative traditions. Kunz, "Pluralism of Legal and Value Systems and International Law," 49 *American Journal of International Law* 370 (1955); Northrop, *The Taming of Nations* (1952); Jenks, *The Common Law of Mankind*, 63-172 (1958); for some strictures upon attempts to solve the problems, see Falk and Mendlovitz, "Some Criticisms of C. Wilfred Jenks' Approach to International Law," 14 *Rutgers Law Review* 1, 4-16 (1959), and McDougal and Lasswell, "The Identification and Appraisal of Diverse Systems of Public Order," in *Studies in World Public Order*, 3-41 (1960).

self-restraint nor Soviet forbearance is probable. Once the satellites are in orbit, a cycle of friction and retaliation is likely to begin.

Adjudication is formally possible. The issue could be put in justiciable form: are observational satellites forbidden by international law? The negative considerations that are applicable to legislation apply *a fortiori* to adjudication. In addition, the Soviet Union refuses to allow legal order to emerge from supranational decisions; it takes a very conservative view of transfers of sovereign discretion. Finally, the establishment of a legal regime for outer space is a polycentric issue ill-suited for adjudicative techniques and institutions.[21] The indefinite nature of the basis for any possible decision tends to undermine its acceptability to the losing litigant. Nations generally refuse to submit important legal controversies to adjudicative organs when they cannot, in advance, envision the general character of the legal solution. In any event, the status of the surveillance program implies a determination of an entire legal regime for outer space. This assumes a scope of inquiry and decision that is not normally possible in the judicial process.

An alternative to a formal decision is to accept the effectiveness of the claim to orbit the satellites as a criterion of its legitimacy. Thus, the United States is not forbidden to orbit observation satellites, but neither is the Soviet Union forbidden to shoot them down. *The Harvard Law Review* in a perceptive note phrased it this way:

> . . . whether the Soviet Union will choose to destroy American spy satellites when it becomes capable of doing so depends on Soviet national goals as conceived by the Soviet leaders. For the purpose of a legal analysis, however, *it is sufficient to observe that whatever the*

---

[21] Fuller, "Adjudication and the Rule of Law," *Proceedings of the American Society of International Law* 1, (1960); Morris "Peace through Law: The Role and Limits of Adjudication," *Id.* at 8.

> *Soviet Union does in this regard will not appear to be violative of international law . . . .* [22]

Reliance upon effective control, as a determinant of the legitimacy of "military" claims, is an undesirable way to fill a legislative vacuum. It tends to accentuate the formative role of relative power in international affairs. The small nations who lack space technology are then left without protection. This further promotes the bipolarization of outer space, since only the United States and the Soviet Union possess the technological base for extensive space activity in the immediate future. It also makes coercive conflict an institutional technique for accommodation; this may be a last resort, but it is hardly acceptable if any alternatives can be found.

A voluntaristic theory of international obligation, as formulated by the *Lotus* majority decision, provides one line of analysis.[23] The basic idea is that the objecting state has the burden of showing that the defendant state acted in violation of an existing rule of international law. Affirmatively speaking, this means that a state may do whatever it is not expressly forbidden to do by international law. Thus, in areas where there is no consensus as to the existence of a legal rule, a state may do whatever it pleases, subject only to another state's right to act in self-defense. Specifically, the United States may launch its observational satellites and the Russians may shoot them down if they *purport* to do so in self-defense.[24] The *Lotus* approach, when coupled with the customary right of self-defense, seems rather similar to the solution reached by the dynamics of effective control. The 1960 U-2 incident suggests that such approaches lead to serious intensifications of Cold

---

[22] Note, "National Sovereignty of Outer Space," 74 *Harvard Law Review* 1154, 1174 (1961). Emphasis supplied.

[23] Case of the SS "Lotus," PCIJ, Ser. A. No. 10 (1927).

[24] In other words, self-determined self-defense is a primary attribute of a decentralized legal order. International law allows a state to characterize, in the first instance, its coercive conduct as "self-defense." This is partly a consequence of the absence of a definition of aggression.

War tensions and interfere with whatever prospects exist for wider accommodations.[25] In addition, we question the legality and wisdom of authorizing a defensive force to test "the permissibility" of the Samos-Midas satellites. The UN Charter's renunciation of force is qualified by Article 51 that preserves "the inherent right of individual or collective self-defense if an armed attack occurs." Certainly, the observational satellite does not constitute "an armed attack." Some Charter experts do contend that Article 51 preserves "the inherent right" that includes a decentralized determination of what must be done in self-defense.[26] It is contended here, however, that such a broad interpretation of the right of self-defense is less plausible than is the narrower alternative. Recourse to a pre-Charter idea of self-defense also gives up a fairly objective standard for the use of defensive force. The need for stable limits on the use of force in a world of nuclear weapons suggests the extreme seriousness of a course of action that allows a victim state no real alternative to the use of defensive force. With this thought in mind, American policy-makers should consider carefully the advisability of presenting the Soviet Union with a situation in which their vital interests can be protected only by a recourse to force.

What is the relevance of the Cold War to the quest for legitimacy in controversial areas of world affairs? The observation satellite controversy raises directly such issues of relevance, since it obviously deals with the perceived vital interests

---

[25] Formalized expressions of public opinion—for instance, resolutions of censure in the United Nations—deserve the status of a weak sanction in the international legal system. Over-analogy, however, to the effectiveness of censure and ridicule in primitive societies is deceptive. We must not forget how much such sanctions depend upon a fairly high level of social integration among members of the community. A lack of just such integration is a major deficiency of the international order. Thus, we must be careful about the analogies between decentralized primitive societies and the decentralized international legal order.

[26] E.g. Stone, *Aggression and World Order* (1958); Stone, *Quest for Survival* (1961).

of the bloc leaders in the Cold War. How much is legitimacy worth to us in our dealings with the Russians? Should we ignore legal restraints in order to meet the Communist challenge? The attitude of Admiral Ward is at one end of the spectrum:

> Isn't it about time to free ourselves of our deception that accommodations can buy peace from the Communists, and that peace with them can be secured through law—even space law? [27]

Observance of law, then, is a matter of unilateral self-restraint for the United States, since there is no mutuality of commitment. The Soviets manipulate legal obligations to suit their political objectives and repudiate such obligations when their objectives change. The United States, in contrast, adheres to all legal obligations once undertaken and thus loses flexibility in the political struggle. According to Ward's view, legal restraint does not restrict Soviet freedom of action, but it does restrict ours. Therefore, we should eschew legal accommodations with the Russians on Cold War issues, since law acts as a trap. Presumably, then, the United States should go briskly forward with its surveillance program regardless of its destabilizing consequences, because Soviet ideology and practice make legal accommodation self-destructive. Law and survival act at cross purposes in the present world.

A more moderate attitude toward the role of law in the Cold War gives critical emphasis to strategy and experience. Legal accommodation may be desirable, but only when we have enough experience to assess the bearing of a legal obligation upon our special needs for survival under present conditions. Loftus Becker, writing as Legal Adviser, said:

> . . . [A]ny sound body of law is based on a system of experience and known facts. There are a great deal

---

[27] "International Control of Outer Space," *Hearings Before the House Committee on Science and Astronautics*, 86th Cong., 1st Sess., 107 (1959) (Testimony of Admiral Ward).

of facts that we just don't know at the present time with respect to outer space and the conditions there existing.[28]

To this uncertainty arising from inexperience is added a deep distrust of the Soviet Union. For instance, Professor Lipson writes:

> In this field [of outer space] as in other fields of international law, Soviet doctrine combines a pious attachment to the names of traditional concepts with a flexible, "instrumental" manipulation of the *content* of the concepts to serve the current needs of Soviet policy.[29]

Distrust leads to an insistence on very clear lines of commitment; hence, we must be sure what we are giving up before we agree with the Russians. In outer space, we lack sufficient experience at present to be sure whether or not a commitment we make today might place us in handcuffs tomorrow. Here again, primacy is given to political factors, and survival is linked to freedom of choice rather than to stable limits upon choice. Law must be content with a marginal role of stabilizing areas of convergence after the facts are assessed rather than with the more ambitious role of preparing an ordering scheme for the emerging facts. In the interim, the *Lotus* style of interpreting sovereignty serves to vindicate all non-prohibited conduct. Existing law does not pertain to outer space. A state can thus do whatever it wants. Therefore, if the surveillance program is helpful to us, we should use it. Much can be said for an approach that is so simple and permissive; however, it fails to take account of the destabilizing effect of *novel unilateral military* claims in a decentralized social order in which the chief actors possess thermonuclear bombs. It also overlooks the horizontal and provisional ordering possibilities that arise from unilateral self-restraint. These possibilities will

---

[28] Becker, *id.* at 75.
[29] See Lipson, *op. cit. supra,* note 18 at 12.

not always gain more order, but they may postpone friction and induce reciprocal self-restraint by the Soviet Union. We would have the choice between surrender and preventive war if we did not posit a minimum Soviet commitment to world order and to the avoidance of nuclear devastation. We often act, however, as if there were few alternatives in the middle. It is rational to take some risks to give order to international relations even though these risks may conceivably accrue to the strategic benefit of the Soviet Union.

At the other end of the spectrum, we find a variety of scholars and concerned public officials who feel that we must establish a vertical legal regime prior to the further assertion of national claims. For instance, Senator Keating stated it in these terms:

> There will be no time for legal craftsmanship and judicial speculation after rival claims are made to the moon or to space itself . . . . The rule of law in the age of space is not a matter of philosophy, but a matter of survival.[30]

Also, John Cobb Cooper has for years brought the weight of his learning and authority to bear in this direction. In 1960, he said at Leiden that "international peace and the future welfare of mankind demand that the Rule of Law shall be applicable with certainty to outer space."[31] A clear agreement as to the rights and duties of nations in outer space is required.

> If the Rule of Law is to be applied in outer space, then I submit, as I have on other occasions, that the area of outer space must be determined, that its legal status be agreed upon, that the rights of States in the areas be universally acknowledged and that the legal

---

[30] See, *op. cit. supra*, note 27 at 2-3 (Testimony of Senator Keating).
[31] Cooper, "Questions of Space Law," 3 *Spaceflight* 95 (1961).

status of flight instrumentalities to be used in outer space be also fixed.[32]

This position stressed the ordering role of law and does so without regard to the existing character of the international system. Without techniques for social change, nations are unwilling to agree on a fixed legal regime until they clearly see what is involved. Space and flight developments have proceeded with such rapidity that those who propose a basis for legal agreement have constantly had to revise their recommendations. Mr. Cooper's writings through the years provide a prominent illustration of the need to change law in order to meet new technological developments.[33] Agreement at any stage is inadequate at the next technological stage; renegotiation is always difficult as a new development has an unequal bearing upon the national interests of the participating states. This feature of non-negotiability would apply most vividly when extra-legal developments have an unequal effect on the military position of the Cold War rivals. Verticalized norms —that is, norms with the formal status of supranational obligations—could not withstand such a strain. It is probably premature, as Becker and Lipson suggest, to create vertical norms to govern outer space at this time. But the search for horizontal legal order is never premature. The alternatives are too often perceived to be either comprehensive international agreement or chaos, either vertical law or lawlessness, either legal restraint or sovereign unrestraint.

My argument is that the effects of the surveillance program upon the stability of the use of outer space, as well as upon the use of defensive force, challenge the rationality of the claims of the United States to use outer space for the military

---

[32] *Ibid.*

[33] Cooper, "Flight-Space, and the Satellites," 7 *International and Comp. Law Quarterly* 2 (1958); Cooper, "High Altitude Flight and National Sovereignty," 4 *International Law Quarterly* 411 (1951); Cooper, "Legal Problems of Upper Space," 1956 *Proc. American Society International Law* 85; Cooper, "Sovereignty in Space," *Flying* (January 1959).

observation of the Soviet Union. Horizontal legal order focuses the inquiry upon the reasonableness of a national claim, given all relevant considerations including infringements upon the interests of other states. This process of inquiry, as outlined here, should influence the decision whether or not to orbit controversial satellites above Soviet territory. Final appraisal rests heavily upon access to data that is unavailable to the public: the importance of the information obtainable, the degree of Soviet objection, the probable success of Soviet attempts to shoot down or otherwise interfere with the satellites, the bearing upon cooperative developments of space, and its eventual contribution to intelligence work. It is discouraging that newspaper reports and legislative hearings reveal no consideration of the wider implications of the space observation program for world order. The strategic advantage of closing the intelligence gap is accepted as a self-sufficient justification for asserting the unilateral claim. Such a foreshortening of inquiry, which seems to underrate the effect of the Samos-Midas program upon international order, is unforgivable in a world where potential enemies in thermonuclear war boast of their "over-kill" capacity. It may be part of the complexity of the times to acknowledge the importance of Henry Kissinger's remark that ". . . the very intensity of our desire for peace may increase our peril." [34] But such a perception should not cause us to deny the firm rationality from which such intensity derives. We must continue to bring our energies to bear in order to diminish our peril.

---

[34] Kissinger, "Nuclear Testing and the Problems of Peace," 37 *Foreign Affairs* 1 (1958).

6

Robert K. Woetzel

LEGAL ASPECTS OF MILITARY USES OF SPACE IN SOVIET AND AMERICAN EYES

The possibility of using space for military purposes has been clear since the launching of the first Soviet ICBMs. At that time the then Secretary of State, John Foster Dulles, attempted to achieve the limitation of the uses of space for peaceful purposes.[1] This effort was frustrated by the Soviet leaders who maintained that Dulles' proposals amounted to a thinly disguised attempt to ban Soviet ICBM weapons while the United States maintained its arsenal in other fields. The Soviet Union suggested linking the problem of peaceful uses of outer space with the question of abandonment of U.S. overseas bases.[2] These proposals were not accepted, and both the United States and the Soviet Union have continued to use space for military purposes.

[1] See *The New York Times*, January 7, 1958, p. 4.

[2] See N. S. Khrushchev, "Speech at the Conference of Foremost Byellorussian Republic Agricultural Personnel," January 22, 1958, *The Current Digest of the Soviet Press*, March 5, 1958, p. 20. In the same vein the leading Soviet space jurist, Prof. Ye. Korovin, stated in "International Status of Cosmic Space," *International Affairs*, January 1959, p. 57, that "The meaning of the U.S. proposal to 'neutralize' the cosmos comes down in practice to forbidding the Soviet intercontinental ballistic missile and represents an attempt to artificially single out the intercontinental missile from the general context of disarmament . . . By proposing to outlaw the intercontinental missile alone, the U.S. rulers seek to head off a retaliatory blow via outer space in the event of an atomic war, while simultaneously retaining numerous military bases on foreign territories."

1. *Types of Space Weapons Systems*

The problem posed by the military uses of space has become more complex with the development of space weapons technologies. The two major space powers, the United States and the Soviet Union, have accumulated great stockpiles of ICBMs. Even though ICBMs do not serve only space functions, but are usually aimed at targets on earth, they can be considered a space weapons system, since they fly, at least briefly, at very high altitudes. Former President Eisenhower declared in a letter to former Soviet Premier Bulganin of January 1958 that "Both the Soviet Union and the United States are now using outer space for the testing of missiles designed for military purposes." [3] Furthermore, both countries have exploded nuclear devices at high altitudes. The United States has held tests at up to five hundred miles in space. The results could be of significance from a military standpoint. The United States has also used such space satellites as Samos and Midas for observation purposes. A primary objective of the Samos satellite was said to be the photographing of military installations in Soviet-bloc countries. The Samos II probably also carried infra-red sensors for detection of missile launches and automatic cameras to expose a large amount of photographic field. The main mission of the Midas was indicated as the detection of rocket launches by use of special infra-red sensors. The U.S. Tiros, Aeros and Cosmos are "weather satellites" which can also be useful for military purposes.

Space weapons systems may be divided into several categories: 1) weapons which are based on earth and are aimed at targets on earth but which pass through space on their way; 2) weapons which are based on earth and are aimed at targets in space; 3) weapons which are based in space and may be directed at targets on earth; 4) weapons which are based in space and may be aimed at targets in space; 5) weapons which represent a combination of two or more of these types.

---

[3] U.S. *Department of State Bulletin*, January 27, 1958, p. 122.

At the present time the first and second categories are most relevant to the discussion on military uses of space.

In the future space may be used for the development of advanced space weapons systems, such as neutron flux weapons, laser-directed nuclear energy which might reduce warning times to a second or so, plasma jets heated millions of degrees into the fourth state of matter, and ionized gas usually known as ball lightning which can be directed by radio at great velocities. So-called evironmental countervalue uses, such as area bursts of large metagon or small gigaton weapons in space to burn large areas of a continent as a terror weapon, might also become of significance for military purposes. The use of these weapons defensively to destroy ICBMs and IRBMs during their passage through space would have the most serious effects on military planning. They could destroy an opponent's deterrent force for all practical purposes by neutralizing its usefulness and would render ICBMs and to some extent IRBMs obsolete. Some of these uses are more futuristic than others; but the examples given should sufficiently demonstrate the power potential of space weaponry.[4]

2. *The Legality of Military Uses of Space*

The purpose of this paper is to consider different Soviet and American viewpoints on the legal implications of the military uses of space in the context of interaction between science and technology on the one side and law and politics on the

---

[4] For detailed discussions of weapons technologies with regard to space, see C.C. Abt, "The Problems and Possibilities of Space Arms Control," *Journal of Arms Control*, January 1963; R.S. Rochlin, *Observation Satellites for Arms Control Inspection* (Schenectady, N.Y.: General Electric Company, 1962); A.H. Katz, "Observation Satellites: Problems and Prospects," *Astronautics*, October 1960; "Missile and Space Activities," *Joint Hearings Before the Preparedness Investigating Subcommittee on Armed Services and the Committee on Astronautical and Space Sciences*, U.S. Senate, 1959; and "Report of the Conference of Experts for the Study of Possible Measures Which Might be Helpful in Preventing Surprise Attack and for the Preparation of a Report Thereon to Governments," *U.N. Doc.* A/4078, S/4145.

other. It is clear that military uses may be developed in accordance with scientific and technological advances. These in turn have certain effects on the policies of countries in the fields of law and diplomacy. The legal situation is, therefore, largely dependent on the scientific progress. This is especially the case in the area of arms control in outer space, as will be shown.

Senator Albert Gore presented the U.S. position on military uses of space before the First Committee at the Seventeenth Session of the U.N. General Assembly on December 3, 1962. Referring to U.S. observation satellites he stated that "Observation from space is consistent with international law, just as is observation from the high seas." His view was largely based on an analogy between outer space and the high seas. Military uses of the high seas are, of course, allowed. The United States favors discusing the limitation of military activities in space in the context of arms control and disarmament.[5]

Mr. Morozov, replying for the Soviet Union, stated that ". . . no analogy exists here with principles applying to the open seas." With reference to U.S. reconnaissance satellites over Russian territory the Soviet delegate declared that "Such gathering of intelligence data through the use of space vehicles is in violation of the sovereign rights of States, and if outer space is to be used in peaceful co-operation, such operations cannot be regarded as legal, or in conformity with international law." He indicated that certain uses of space had more dangerous consequences than similar uses on the high seas. The Soviet Union has favored a declaration which would ban certain activities in space like the sending of reconnaisance satellites and the use of space instrumentalities for war propaganda.[6]

---

[5] Senator Gore's speech in *U.N. Doc.* A/C.1/P.V. 1289; see also paper on "Observation in Space" by Leonard Meeker, delivered at a Conference on Urgent Problems of Space Law at McGill University, Montreal, on April 13, 1963 (Typescript) now printed in Cohen, ed., *Law and Politics in Space* (Montreal: McGill U. Press, 1964).

[6] Mr. Morozov's speech in *U.N. Doc.* A/C.1/P.V. 1289; see also Draft Declaration of the Basic Principles governing the Activities of

In Resolution 1472, adopted on December 12, 1959, the U.N. General Assembly recognized "the common interest of mankind as a whole in furthering the peaceful use of outer space," and expressed the wish "to avoid the extension of present national rivalries into this new field." In Resolution 1721, adopted on December 20, 1961 ,the United Nations recognized "the common interest of mankind in furthering the peaceful use of outer space" and for "the betterment of man" and for the benefit of all countries without regard to their stage of development. These resolutions clearly indicate that it is the wish of the international community to avoid the extension of national rivalries into space.[7]

In particular, it must be determined what kind of rivalries would be contrary to the wishes of the international community. Peaceful uses of space are clearly allowed according to the U.N. resolutions, and no state has objected to the flight of scientific satellites like Explorer and Sputnik over its territory. It may be assumed, therefore, that states have the right to utilize space and the celestial bodies for peaceful scientific, economic and social purposes.[8] The policy declarations of most governments in the course of the United Nations debates indicate that national rivalries involving non-peaceful uses of

States in the Exploration and Use of Outer Space submitted by the U.S.S.R., *U.N. Doc.* A/AC.105/C.2/L.6. The problem of so-called "spy satellites" is complicated by the fact that the U.S. makes a public policy out of sending them. Spying during peacetime represents an anomaly in international relations indulged in by states under a cloak of secrecy. It has not hitherto been claimed by states that they have a "right" to spy. The assertion by the U.S. government makes such "observation" an Act of State which the U.S.S.R. claims is in violation of its sovereign rights.

[7] See discussion in R.K. Woetzel, *Die internationale Kontrolle der hoeheren Luftschichten und des Weltraums* (hereafter referred to as *The International Control of Space*) (Bad Godesberg: Asgard Verlag, 1960), pp. 57-63.

[8] See discussion in Woetzel, "Sovereignty and National Rights in Outer Space and on Celestial Bodies," *Proceedings of the Vth Colloquium on the Law of Outer Space* (Washington, D.C.: International Institute of Space Law, 1963), pp. 24-34.

space should be avoided. Many authors have equally opposed the use of space for other than peaceful purposes.[9]

A complicating factor, however, is the question whether peaceful uses refer to *non-aggressive* or *non-military* uses. If only aggressive uses are forbidden, then military uses may still be allowed. In this sense Senator Gore explained in his statement to the First Committee last December that "It is the view of the United States that outer space should be used only for peaceful—that is, non-aggressive and beneficial—purposes . . . the test of any space activity must not be whether it is military or non-military, but whether or not it is consistent with the United Nations Charter and other obligations of international law." The United States regards the observation satellites as essentially "peaceful" in character, because they enhance international security by creating an open society and diminishing the danger of surprise attack.

From the discussions in the legal sub-committee of the United Nations Committee on the Peaceful Uses of Outer Space it is clear that the nations do not favor the extension of the arms race into space.[10] It appears, therefore, that at this time space cannot be compared to the high seas in the sense that military uses are clearly allowed like on the high seas. While space is open for peaceful exploration by all states, according to U.N. Resolutions 1472 and 1721, uses of space for military

---

[9] Sir L.K. Munro, "The Control of Outer Space and the United Nations," in *Space Law—A Symposium*, Special Committee on Space and Astronautics, U.S. Senate, 1959, p. 380; C. Horsford, "Principles of International Law in Space Flight," *St. Louis University Law Journal*, 1958, p. 78; and C.S. Rhyne, "The Legal Horizons of Space Use and Exploration," *Congressional Record*, 1958, p. 6154, among others.

[10] See, for example, the Draft Code for International Cooperation in the Peace Uses of Outer Space of the United Arab Republic, *U.N. Doc.* A/AC.105/L6; and compare to Draft Declaration of Basic Principles Governing the Activities of States pertaining to the Exploration and Use of Outer Space submitted by the United Kingdom, *U.N. Doc.* A/C.1/879; Draft Declaration of Principles relating to the Exploration and Use of Outer Space submitted by the U.S.A., *U.N. Doc.* A/C.1/881; and Draft Declaration submitted by the U.S.S.R. referred to in note 6 *supra*.

purposes have not been approved by the international community. Space can, therefore, be considered *res communis* with certain limitations.[11]

As has been indicated the U.N. resolutions are not clear on whether the word peaceful refers to non-military or non-aggressive uses of space; a more explicit resolution outlawing military uses of space or even an international treaty would be required to provide an international standard for the exploration and use of outer space. General Assembly resolutions are not formally binding on states, although they express the wishes of the international community; a treaty like the Kellogg-Briand Pact which made illegal the recourse to war as an instrument of national policy might, therefore, be preferable from the standpoint of establishing a principle of international law. A most general definition of the term military would suffice for a declaration outlawing military uses of space, such as: any activity in space which is essentially military in character, because it serves the military establishment of a country, adds to its weapons arsenal, and extends the arms race into outer space. Activities which are essentially non-military in character, but whose by-products might be useful to military authorities, e.g. weather information, would not be included in this definition.

It is not necessary to formulate enumerative definitions of terms like military and aggressive to suit all possible circumstances, in order to apply them in specific cases. In the past, the U.S.S.R. has favored an enumerative definition of aggression. The International Military Tribunal at Nuremberg, however, applied the general concept of aggression in judging cases involving crimes against peace, and this was endorsed by the United Nations.[12] Similarly, a general definition of mili-

---

[11] See Woetzel, *The International Control of Space*, p. 61 *et seq.*
[12] Woetzel, *The Nuremberg Trials in International Law* (Second Revised Edition with a Postlude on the Eichmann Trial) (London and New York: Stevens and Praeger, 1962) pp. 154-172.

tary uses of space could be applied from case to case. This would not rule out specific agreements not to engage in certain activities in space. In fact, the history of air law shows that the general principles of the Paris Convention of 1919 and the Chicago Convention of 1944 were supplemented by special agreements; thus, for example, the general principle of "innocent passage" was subsequently qualified by the Two Freedoms Agreement.[13]

A ban on military activities could serve different objectives: it might prohibit any conceivable military use of space; or it might forbid the further extension of the arms race into space. In the latter case the control of existing space weapons might be left to the disarmament negotions. A country which violates a general declaration not to use space for military purposes would forfeit its benefits under the pact, and states would be entitled to react in kind. The country which started the chain reaction would incur the onus of disapproval of the international community.

---

[13] Concerning the usefulness of a general definition see also Oppenheim-Lauterpacht, *International Law* (London: Longmans, Green and Co., 1955), Vol. II, p. 189: "It is commonly, but erroneously, assumed that the adoption of a definition of aggression necessarily deprives governments or tribunals of the freedom of appreciation of the merits of a particular situation. No definition acts automatically. It must always be a matter for a judicial tribunal, or a State, or any other agency entitled to form a judgment, to apply the elements of the definition to the case before it. . . . Definitions represent that element of certainty in the operation and observance of the law which is no less essential in international relations than within the State. A definition of aggression may also be instrumental in making it more difficult for States to pursue a policy of treating the conception of self-defense as identical with the defense of any interest to which they attach importance." Likewise a general definition of the term "military" might discourage nations from engaging upon enterprises which obviously fall into this category like, for example, the placing of weapons in orbit. In that connection see statement by Leonard Meeker, *op. cit.*, p. 14: "Even though it is now feasible to do so, the United States has no intention of placing such weapons in orbit unless compelled to do so by actions of the Soviet Union."

A real obstacle to practical enforcement of such a declaration would be the difficulty of determining the purpose to which space vehicles are being put, whether essentially military or non-military in character, which is discussed hereafter in connection with the problem of arms control and disarmament on earth and in space. Nevertheless, a ban on military uses might help to create an atmosphere which would mitigate against the extension of the arms race into space by serving as a "guideline" to policy-makers. In that connection it might be well to remember the words of Mr. Leonard Meeker, Deputy Legal Adviser of the U.S. State Department, at a conference in Montreal in April, 1963: ". . . it is clearly easier *not to arm* a part of the environment that has never been armed than to *disarm* parts that have been armed."[14]

3. *The Legality of the Threat or Use of Force in Space*

While it is controversial at the present time whether the term non-peaceful refers to non-military or non-aggressive uses, Article 2(4) of the U.N. Charter unequivocally calls upon all members to ". . . refrain in their international relations from the threat or use of force against the territorial integrity or political independence of any state." Consequently, any use involving the threat or use of force is not permitted according to the Charter. Article 51 qualifies this by granting states the ". . . inherent right of individual or collective self-defence if an armed attack occurs. The threat or use of force is not allowed, therefore, except in exercise of the right of self-defence in case of armed attack. According to U.N. Resolution 1721 these principles apply to outer space as on earth.

Two broad categories of defence actions are possible under this system: 1) individual or collective self-defence against an armed attack directed from or through outer space at an object on earth; 2) individual or collective self-defence

---

[14] Meeker, *op. cit.* (note 5).

against an armed atack directed from or through outer space at an object in space. In either case, a nation would have the right to use force to repell the attack. The fact that Resolution 1721 states that outer space and the celestial bodies are not open for "national appropriation" would not affect the right of a state to defend its citizens and property in space against an armed attack. Furthermore, an attack taking place from or through outer space would automatically release states from any obligation not to arm in this area.

It has been maintained by certain writers that states may use or threaten force against actions of other countries which they consider a threat to their security, even if they do not involve an armed attack. Thus the Soviet jurist Zadorozhnyi states that "The right of a state to destroy a satellite-spy and in general every space device whatsoever interfering with the security of this state is indisputable." [15] The American law professor McDougal has maintained in a similar vein that "If it is felt by an underlying state that the passing spacecraft endangers its security, it is going to shoot it down if it can." [16] In his opinion this would not necessarily conflict with an analogy between space and the high seas as mentioned by Senator Gore, since the United States among other countries has asserted the right to protect itself against threats to its security on the high seas and in the skies above the oceans on the basis of "continguity" even though these areas are regarded as *res communis* in international law. The Air Defense Identification Zones established by the United States reach out far beyond the three mile limit above the high seas.[17]

---

[15] G.P. Zadorozhnyi, "Basic Problems of the Science of Space Law," *The Cosmos and International Law*, ed. by Ye. Korovin (Moscow: Institut Mezhdunarodnykh Otnosheniy, 1962), p. 53.

[16] M.S. McDougal in *Proceedings of the American Society of International Law*, April 25-28, 1956.

[17] See also U.S. Rear Admiral C. Ward, "Projecting the Law of the Sea into the Law of Space," *The JAG Journal*, March 1957, p. 4 *et seq.*

Regardless of whether states have acquiesced in these particular claims by the United States, the unilateral assertion of a right by a state does not establish a generally recognized principle of law, nor are the rights of other countries under customary or conventional international law invalidated thereby. Policy decisions do not necessarily make law; the decision of the Nazi policy makers to wage war was as little in accordance with international law as the unilateral use of force would be under the U.N. Charter, except in case of self-defence or exercise of an international mandate. States are free to explore and use space for peaceful purposes, as has been indicated; but the right to use force in space as on earth is clearly restricted by the U.N. Charter and the general principles of international law. If a nation considers the actions of another country a threat to its security, even if it does not involve an armed attack, it should submit the matter to the United Nations. According to Article 39 of the Charter, the Security Council can curb actions which amount to a " . . . threat to the peace, breach of the peace, or an act of aggression." And according to Article 11, the General Assembly may also make recommendations with regard to the " . . . general principles of co-operation in the maintenance of international peace and security."

Explaining the U.S. position in this regard, Mr. Meeker has stated that "The standards which must be used in determining and controlling exertions of national power have not been altered by the new world which outer space activities has opened to us all. . . . (They) remain those set forth in the Charter of the United Nations. Article 2, paragraph 4 imposes the obligation to refrain from the threat or use of force . . . Article 2, paragraph 3 imposes the obligation to settle international disputes by peaceful means . . . The principles laid down in the Charter set the limits of permissible State conduct." [18]

---

[18] Meeker, *op. cit.*, note 5, at p. 15.

Only under extremely exceptional circumstances would a state be justified in using force except under the conditions indicated above. This might be the case if the international peace-keeping machinery proved totally inadequate as with the League of Nations, or if a state was faced by a threat of attack instant and overwhelming, leaving no moment for deliberation or other recourse, to use the classic definition of circumstances justifying action in self-defence by Secretary of State Webster in the Caroline case. [19] In the nuclear age, when weapons may be delivered in a matter of minutes or even seconds and a country's counter-strike capability can be paralyzed as a result, the time factor may be of crucial importance. Under such extreme circumstances a nation could be expected to fall back on a claim to an inherent right of self-defence and self-protection. But this would not preclude censure and judgment by an organ representing the international community like the United Nations, or for that matter, individual responsibility for crimes against peace. Politicians are not above the law as the Nuremberg trials have shown. The power to assert a certain standard or effective control does not alter this fact. Might does not make right in space or on earth! [20]

---

[19] See 2 Moore, *International Law* 24-30 (1906); *People* v. *McLeod*, 25 Wend. 481 (N. Y., 1841). See also the judgment of the International Military Tribunal at Nuremberg in *The Trial of the Major War Criminals before the International Military Tribunal*, Nuremberg 1948, Vol. XXII, p. 450: ". . . preventive action in foreign territory is justified only in case of an *instant and overwhelming necessity for self-defense, leaving no choice of means, and no moment of deliberation.*" (Italics mine)

[20] This notwithstanding Myres S. McDougal's theory which has recently been summarized in an eloquent critique by Stanley V. Anderson as "Law is policy. Policy is human dignity. Human dignity is fostered in the long run by the success of American foreign policy. Therefore, law is the handmaiden of the national interest of the United States. (Other countries will substitute their own national policy in place of the American.)" "A Critique of Professor Myres S. McDougal's Doctrine of Interpretation by Major Purposes," *American Journal of International Law*, April, 1963, p. 382. See also Woetzel, *The Nuremberg Trials in International Law*, "Crimes against Peace," pp. 122-171.

The question of the boundary line between air and space can be of great importance in connection with the problem of military uses of space. A nation may exercise complete and exclusive jurisdiction in its sovereign airspace, according to the Paris and Chicago Conventions.[21] This means that it can prevent trespass. On the other hand, U.N. Resolution 1721 states that space shall not be open for national appropriation. Neither the United States nor the Soviet Union have claimed sovereignty in space, and the majority of authors are opposed to such claims.[22] It would be difficult to envisage cones of sovereignty projected from earth *usque ad coelum,* since celestial bodies would be moving from one cone into the other according to the immutable laws of the universe.[23] The question as to where exclusive jurisdiction of a nation in its sovereign airspace ends

---

[21] Article 1 of the Paris Convention states that "The High Contracting Parties recognize that every Power has complete and exclusive sovereignty over the air space above its territory." The Chicago Convention contains a similar provision.

[22] See O. Schachter, "Who Owns the Universe?" in *Across the Space Frontier,* 1952; W. H. V. Hanover, *Lufrecht und Weltraum* (Goettingen University, 1953); C. Horsford, "The Law of Space," *Journal of the British Interplanetary Society,* May-June, 1955, pp. 144-150; P. Jessup and H. Taubenfeld, *Controls for Outer Space and the Antarctic Analogy* (New York: Columbia University Press, 1959); C. W. Jenks, "International Law and Activities in Space," *International Law and Comparative Law Quarterly,* January 1956, pp. 99-114; D. B. Craig, "National Sovereignty at High Altitudes,"*Journal of Air Law and Commerce,* Autumn 1957, pp. 384-597; G. P. Zadorozhnyi, "The Artificial Satellite and International Law," *Sovetskaya Rossiya,* 1957; N. Mateesco, "A qui appartient le milieu aerien?" *Revue du barreau de la Province de Quebec,* May 1952, pp. 227-242; J. Kroell, "Elements createurs d'un droit astronautique," *Revue generale de l'air,* 1953, pp. 222-245; A. Meyer, "Bemerkungen zu dem Vortrag von Prof. Cooper, Legal Problems in Upper Space," *Zeitschrift fuer Luftrecht,* 1956, pp. 180-183; K. H. Boehme, "Lufthoheit und Weltraumflug," *Zeitschrift fuer Luftrecht,* 1956, pp. 184-197; M. Smirnoff, "La reglementation internationale des voes dans l'espace supra-atmospherique," *Revue generale de l'air,* 1957, pp. 347-351; and P. L. Bret, "Le control de l'espace," *Revue generale de l'air,* 1958, pp. 3-9, among others.

[23] For discussion of this subject see Woetzel, "Sovereignty and National Rights in Outer Space and on Celestial Bodies," *op. cit.,* pp. 3-23.

and outer space begins is extremely significant, because a nation might be justified according to international law in using force in its airspace while this would not be the case in outer space, except in self-defence. The Soviet Union can present a good case for interfering with the American U-2 reconnaissance plane in its national airspace, but the destruction of an American satellite in space would have completely different legal significance.

The attempt has been made to determine a limit to national airspace by defining the terms airspace and aircraft. Mr. Loftus Becker, former Legal Adviser to the U.S. State Department, once declared that the fact that air particles could be found at an altitude of 10,000 miles left the United States a lot of "elbow-room for discussion." [24] This would seem to be a rather exaggerated claim, however, in view of the definition of aircraft in Annex 7 to the Chicago Convention as flightcraft "which can derive support in the atmosphere from the reactions of the air." The point at which aerodynamic lift ceases and centrifugal forces takes over is approximately fifty to sixty miles above the earth's surface but ordinary aircraft navigate at much lower altitudes; the American X-15 plane is capable, however, of rising to such heights. While sixty miles is probably a high limit to airspace which the framers of the Chicago Convention had in mind when they drafted Annex 7 and represents the only standard that could be applied for legal purposes at this time, the annexes are not binding and are "for convenience only" according to Article 54(1) of the Convention. [25] There is no agreed boundary between air and space, therefore, at the present time; nor, for that matter, has it been determined definitely what constitutes the difference between aircraft and spacecraft.

---

[24] L. Becker, "Major Aspects of the Problem of Outer Space," *U. S. Department of State Bulletin*, June 9, 1958, p. 965 *et seq.*

[25] See also definition of "aircraft" by the David Davies Memorial Institute Study Group on the Law of Outer Space in "Draft Code of Rules on the Exploration and Uses of Outer Space" as "any craft which depends,

The Polish jurist Sztucki has explained that "Since there is no upper limit of national sovereignty or national jurisdiction, no space activity can be described as carried out below or above such a limit. Under these circumstances a legal qualification can not be based on any special criteria, it may only be functional." [26] Even though there is no agreed boundary line between air and space, this does not give states unlimited rights in the space above their territories. Airspace does not extend indefinitely, and in the absence of clearly defined standards as to what constitutes an air or spacecraft, states must look for guidance to the general principles of international law and the U. N. Charter. They must accordingly avoid the use or threat of force unless clearly justified in case of an incursion into their airspace at low altitudes by aircraft as defined in Annex 8 of the Chicago Convention, or in the face of an armed attack, or in execution of an international mandate. They should refrain from any actions which disturb international peace and impede space exploration and discovery. As to what kind of actions threaten the peace, this would be subject to determination by the United Nations, as explained above.

4. *Military Uses of Space and Arms Control*

The subject of military uses of space is closely related to the problem of arms control. Arms control in space cannot be totally separated from the same problem on earth. This seems to be the position of both the United States and the Soviet Union at the present time. It does not mean, however, that disarmament in space must in all cases be linked to disarmament on earth; the Soviet Union has proposed in the past that a ban on non-peaceful uses of space be connected with

---

as means of flight upon the consumption of air, or upon aerodynamic lift, or both." Airspace begins to lose its character of a continuous medium when a height of 50-55 miles is reached. It suggests an altitude of 50 miles as the limit of sovereignty and the beginning of outer space.

[26] J. Sztucki, "On the So-called Upper Limit of National Sovereignty," (typescript), 1962, pp. 8-9.

the abandonment of U.S. overseas bases. Arms control in space as on earth must be considered functionally, that is in terms of specific military uses. The regulation of a particular use will depend on the factors involved. While the United States and the U.S.S.R. have often disagreed about the need for inspection to verify compacts this has not prevented the Antarctic Treaty of 1959 which provides for a demilitarized zone and inspection.[27] Furthermore, the United States recently demonstrated that it did not insist on inspection for a moratorium on certain nuclear tests and there are thus no international inspection provisions in the partial Nuclear Test Ban Treaty dealing with tests in the atmosphere, in outer space or under the seas. The refinement of scientific means for verification have apparently made "on-the-site" inspection unnecessary in such cases. Similarly, agreements on further arms control in space will require different formulae depending on the function of a particular military use and the factors involved.

In the past certain U.S. and British proposals for on-the-site inspection have been rejected by the Soviet Union, because this would supposedly amount to a form of espionage, among other reasons. Similar objections might be encountered with regard to on-the-site inspection of Soviet space instrumentalities on launching pads. Premier Khrushchev has indicated, however, that the Soviet Union was not opposed to inspection in principle;[28] whether this will lead to a broad agreement on arms control remains to be seen. As far as inspection in outer space is concerned, no scientific means for this purpose have been devised yet. While it would probably be extremely costly to construct them, it is conceivable that technological advances may make possible adequate inspection or verification

---

[27] According to Article VII of the Antarctic Treaty of 1959 nations participating in the Consultative Conference on the Antarctic can dispatch representatives to any part of the region, in order to inspect stations, equipment, ships and planes at points of loading and unloading.

[28] See *Die Zeit*, February 1, 1963, p. 1.

mechanisms which could transmit information as to the function of a particular instrumentality or installation in outer space. It would still be difficult, however, to determine whether the purpose of a spacecraft or station would be military or non-military as has been pointed out previously; an observatory on the moon, for example, could serve either scientific meteorological or military reconnaissance aims. We now have a General Assembly resolution proposing that weapons of mass destruction not be orbitted and it may eventually be possible to reach other limited agreements not involving inspection.

Until the formula or formulae are devised for ensuring the security of states under conditions of controlled disarmament, the development of weapons technologies in outer space and the use of space for many military purposes are likely to continue. It is to be hoped that further agreements on different areas of arms control will be forthcoming soon, lest the arms race be further extended into space. Scientists including Dr. Van Allan already have warned of the danger to manned space flight of a radiation belt due to high altitude tests. The United States and the Soviet Union bear the primary responsibilities for resolving their differences in this area so that peace may be assured on earth and in space.

In view of the need to guard against possible breaches of arms control agreements, the nations must decide upon a satisfactory detection or inspection system. But suspicions of each others' motives should not be exaggerated to the point that any agreement becomes impossible. A certain line of thinking is opposed to any accommodation between the nations, even when this is for the common good. Some persons are suspicious of cultural contacts, scientific and educational exchanges, and international peaceful co-operation. It would appear as if they believed that what is favored by the other side cannot possibly be in their country's interest; thus if the other side is against nuclear war, because of the danger of total annihilation of mankind, they feel that it might be in their interest to risk a clash of arms. Their thinking is rigid and dangerous; their influence is pernicious. Both the United States and the Soviet Union have repudiated them; but it is necessary to be constantly on guard against them, lest they thwart the efforts to promote international peace.[29]

5. Conclusion

It can be concluded that neither the United States nor the Soviet Union can dictate a regime for outer space which only takes into consideration their respective national interests. Their technological superiority does not entitle them to set standards for the whole world. The international community represented in the United Nations has indicated that space is open for exploration by states for peaceful purposes only. States should, therefore, avoid uses of space which may lead to international conflict. Military uses which constitute breaches or threats to the peace may be brought before the U.N. Security Council. This does not mean that the objections of a state to claims of another state in space are automatically binding; general standards must be applied according to the nature of each case. States may tacitly or expressly agree to claims to use space; but controversial uses which threaten the peace and security of nations should be brought before the United Nations according to Article 24 of the Charter, unless states can reconcile their differences by other means. It might be advisable for states to develop their claims in space by mutual consultation, even if agreement cannot be reached in every instance. In the very least this may serve to lessen international tension by diminishing the shock effect of unilateral assertions of claims.

---

[29] See Pope John XXIII, *Peace on Earth*, reprinted in *Catholic News*, April 18, 1963, p. 6E, Col. 4: "In the highest and most authoritative assemblies, let men give serious thought to the problem of a peaceful adjustment of relations between political communities on a world level—an adjustment founded on mutual trust, on sincerity in negotiations and on faithful fulfillment of obligations assumed. Let them study the problem until they find that point from which it will be possible to commence to go forward toward accords that will be sincere, lasting and fruitful."

The difference between the ideologies and economic systems of the countries cannot be ignored; but they do not constitute insurmountable barriers to agreements for example, on exchanges of meteorological information, liability for damages due to spacecraft, and the safety and rescue of astronauts. Hopefully, nations may also reach enforcible agreements on arms control which extend to space and celestial bodies. The great powers have a limited time within which to reach an understanding before nuclear weapons become part of the arsenal of many countries and the danger of atomic war is increased. In view of innumerable appeals by governments for limitations on arms and international discussions on disarmament the extension of the arms race into space can be regarded clearly contrary to the hopes and expectations of the world community. Even without a declaration expressly outlawing all military uses of space, unilateral exercises of power which extend the arms race into this area have a precedent-setting effect which disturbs international peace by provoking retaliation in kind.

7

Howard J. Taubenfeld

THE STATUS OF COMPETING CLAIMS TO USE OUTER SPACE: AN AMERICAN POINT OF VIEW*

While to date it is national states which have dominated our thinking about space, in a broad sense, claims relating to outer space use have been or may be made by men on their own behalf, or by groups of men acting as scientists or as commercial entities or as national states or as international entities. In their international aspects, only some of the key claims can be resolved or adjusted by international law as we now know it. What are the principal uses of an outer space capability? What is the status of some of the conflicting claims arising from such uses? What groups or entities may be involved in the conflicts of interest which are developing? What institutions and techniques for conflict resolution exist or can be envisaged?

Without doing more than sketch in the range of these questions, we can set out at least seven or eight major uses of outer space subject to competitive dispute. These include a) the scientific investigation of the space environment, the planets and the universe; b) satellite communications systems; c) satellite meteorological and navigation systems; d) satellite observation systems which may be either 1 — scientific, for example, telescopes aimed out at the universe or low resolution cameras aimed toward the earth for cloud cover study,

---

* An earlier version of this paper appears in the 1963 Proceedings of The American Society of International Law at pages 173-186.

or 2—on peace-keeping missions, for example, for warning against surprise attack or as part of an international disarmament inspection system, or 3—on national security and military missions, as for example, for targeting and reconnaissance and information gathering heretofore accomplished largely by such diverse groups as diplomatic agents, peaceful geographers, oceanographers and other scientists, spies and overflights by planes. Near-in space may also be used for e) weapons testing and missile flights — the present ICBM's actually move through space briefly though, theoretically, they need not since space may be so defined as to not include either this activity or the altitudes reached or, alternatively, technology could lower the flight altitude. At present of course, they are a major, if momentary, military user of what we think of as space.

In addition to all these imminent or existent earth-oriented economic, political, military and scientific activities, there are potentially competitive activities which, though of course by and for man, are focused outward and are oriented directly to the use and exploitation of outer space itself and to the spread of national power to the newly opened reaches. These include: f) space-oriented miltary systems as such which use outer space as a principal medium or theatre, for example, testing nuclear weapons, placing such weapons in orbit, or creating military systems on space bases or the celestial bodies. There is also g) the extension of territory or sovereign rights by the addition of claimed sovereignty in outer space or to the celestial bodies. In addition there is a last, very important fruit of space use which is competitively sought with avidity and which leads to claims of various types — national prestige. Space achievement has become an index of technological and scientific prowess and, by implication, of national power. This may be thought of as a dummy variable, representing in fact all other valuable space resources, techniques and uses not now foreseen or foreseeable to many who press costly space projects purely for national prestige reasons. Southeast Asia, as a historical precedent, was claimed by the imperial powers before its rubber and other sources of wealth were foreseen. The powers *knew* the colonies would be useful for something. To avoid an unforeseen, destabilizing technical or political or economic breakthrough by their rivals, great states generally have found that they must stay at the advancing frontier of human knowledge and exploration. It is in this sense that prestige, which reflects superior knowledge and techniques, reflects a genuine capacity to advance and to defend oneself under all circumstances and to get whatever turns out to be worth getting. This is real power and it in turn, yields prestige.

This listing may not be complete but it indicates clearly the magnitude of the potential for eventual conflicts of interest.

II CONFLICTS IN USES AND POINTS OF VIEW

a) *The Scientists*

Let us now follow this sketched list of possibly competitive uses of space and test out the "simpler" cases of conflicts of interests in space, for example, the claims of scientists to an undiminished, undistorted, freely observable outer space. Scientific claims have been raised both generally and with respect to specific projects and their study permits insights into the complexities of even the "simplest" case. Project West Ford, the American attempt to scatter copper needles for communications purposes was vehemently criticized, for example, as a potential interference with scientific observation. Then when other scientists and communications men indicated that this seemed overwrought, it was held up as at least the forerunner of a scientifically undesirable "cluttering up" of space. High altitude nuclear tests have been objected to as distorting the Van Allen belt and making studies of the earth's natural environment difficult and even as a potential menace to man in space. Biologists and others have demanded that vehicles used for exploring celestial bodies not contaminate those bodies with earth forms of life and thus perhaps interfere with studies of life in other environments. Radio astronomers have insisted that a substantial number of the highly valuable, limited number of existing radio frequencies be left free for their exclusive use. This is already at issue in the United States as ground users in the Paterson, New Jersey area compete with radio astronomers for use of a frequency allocation.

Clearly claims of one group of scientists may conflict with those of another. All scientific claims may conflict with the desires of other groups and with other desirable social ends, with those who run radio networks, for example, in the same or in different countries, and who honestly feel that preference for their immediately productive commercial needs is to their own and to the general profit. Furthermore, scientists may have different estimates of the values and the dangers of compromising effects of each others work. Even in supposedly "purely scientific" opinion, these honest differences probably are ultimately not entirely free of the scientists' ethical values and political preferences. In many cases, there seems no other way to explain the diversity of scientific opinion on such issues as the feasibility of the H-bomb, the dangers of radiation from fallout, or needles in space.

As if rational social decision were not difficult enough to reach on the basis of such equivocal information as to relative costs and benefits to society, the needs of scientists and all other potential space users may conflict with asserted requirements of national security in space. This ubiquitous dimension of space activities dominates the rest so, of necessity, we must here indicate our approach, since we are in a world of self-seeking, self-defending national states. The national incentives which have over-ridden the enormous financial barriers to space are military security and national prestige. Useful economic and scientific by-products remain trappings, highly significant trappings, but the costly race into space is engined by the belief, perhaps erroneous, that not only national prestige but, somehow, national survival may be at stake.

For the present the potential interference with scientific activities is not likely to deter a state from any act in space considered vital to this central reason for its being there. High altitude nuclear tests, if they are viewed as important for military purposes, will doubtless be continued, whatever their effect in distorting the scientist's ability to observe natural space phenomena.

We can thus state a first conclusion relevant to all other claims to use space. In our world, the claims which the military choose to stress will, directly or indirectly, come before all other claims. This does not end the subject of course. Claims pressed by others will, hopefully, affect the military both by compressing their choice as to what is truly essential to them and also in the way they pursue their irreducible needs in space. Thus high altitude tests may well be reduced in number or shaped or designed in an effort to produce as little untoward interference as possible, consistent with military needs.

Our "simple" case has thus been helpful. We can now pursue the claims of a few of the other important, interesting, non-strategic users of space and the conflicts of interest amongst themselves both nationally and internationally and their conflicts with military claims even though we recognize realistically the overshadowing status of national strategic claims. Later, we will try to suggest the institutional mechanism by which these conflicting claims have been or are likely to be accommodated with each other and with the overriding claims of the national security and prestige sector. Needed improvements in the established national institutions of decision-making between conflicting socially desirable claims should then become more obvious and so should the need for changes in the present decentralized international decision-making institutions which may be the only possibility for reversing the overriding position of claims based on national self-defense and prestige on earth and in space.

b) *Communications Systems*

Since it involves economic and ideological conflicts of interest, the use of satellite communications systems offers a related but still more difficult case than the claims of scientists. It has aleady presented a broad range of actual and potential domestic and international political clashes. Within the United States, various candidates for the privilege of exploiting a space communications network exist. The debate between proponents of a governmentally owned system and advocates of a communications companies owned or dominated system was not ended even by a filibuster in 1962 which led to the first cloture in the American Senate in 35 years. Charges of a "giveaway" are still heard from those who point to the vast governmental expenditures in developing the launch and scientific systems. The companies point out that space capacity is merely an addition, and eventually a competitive one, to existing world wide communications links and offer their experience and the general social philosophy of the United States that, other things being equal, private ownership implies more efficient and dynamic management.

Stripped of the fanfare, the issues involved in these claims seem to be that a space network, which may greatly cheapen the cost of providing communications services, may represent a new opportunity to provide socially desirable services including the development of service to new, politically important, but not yet profitable areas and the subsidization of educational users. Such services involve profits which are long-run or diffused throughout society and are not normally those which a commercial enterprise would have much incentive to provide. Considering that much of the investment in research and development in boosters is government investment, the right of the general public to control a large share of the profits from innovation is clear and easy to defend. The large federal capital R & D donation to a group of private entrepreneurs in what is in any case a powerful but regulated monopoly industry is easy to label a "giveaway," as are, indeed, other similar government financed and commissioned R & D programs, for example, in developing aircraft from which aircraft and airline companies may gain.

The question then becomes: can government regulation of the end product of its debates, a hybrid, quasi-governmental corporation in a regulated industry induce the socially desired results in terms of service, charges, coverage and new lines of development and other national as well as international needs, all while retaining the advantages of private management? In any case, this is the compromise which won, a structurally awkward private company, with governmental interest expressed in various ways in its charter, with three directors appointed by the President, all incorporators confirmed by the Senate, but, according to the Attorney-General, with none of the directors a public official. And as a postscript, the companies and others involved are having second thoughts about the financial wisdom of their shaded triumph. If the corporation fails in its endeavors, or if the Soviet Union, using a governmentally operated system, beats it, this will indicate that the compromise was poor though not necessarily bad in concept but possibly just premature.

There is another facet to this particular set of claims. Internationally, we may well see non-military systems placed in space by Britain, by a European group such as Eurospace or by the Soviet Union in addition to that launched by the United States. There are also advocates of a United Nations system which might well be devoted to meeting the claims of the developing nations for the dissemination of information, teaching and the like. In this form, it would yield a net cost to the U.N., a social contribution. Others have suggested a broader U.N. system to yield revenues to the U.N. These ideas are fascinating but space prevents their discussion here.

Let us assume that this valuable asset, a space communications network, is set up in duplicate or triplicate without centralized coordination. Conflicts of interest would be inevitable between proponents of the different commercial systems and between them and military or U.N. systems over allocation of the physically scarce resource in question, radio frequencies, on a global basis. For the same reason, there is potential conflict with other claimants such as radio astronomers and ground communications users. Last but not least, there is the potentially more explosive inernational version of a fundamental conceptual conflict which space communications activities has brought to the fore. The Soviet Union contends that only states or international organizations may use outer space; Telstar and the Satellite Communications Corporation mark the debut of private enterprise (more or less) in space.

If the Soviet Union is only concerned with identifying a space vehicle as a state craft for purposes of assigning responsibility for damages caused or for registration, verification or inspection in some form of its peaceful nature, which now seems to be the case, there is no real problem. For national and international security, all vehicles would have to be so considered and included. If Russia is in fact asserting that peaceful, commercial space activities can only be carried out by states, that is a different matter. The scope of purely private ventures in space may be limited for decades because of the heavy capital inputs required but the imposition of a socialist pattern on space activities is unlikely to be acceptable to the United States. Moreover, it has no special precedent in communications where regulated, private, and national systems have commonly co-existed, side by side or, in fact, in other industries exploiting natural resources in other spheres. We will therefore assume that space will not be legally communized.

There is yet another dimension of possible conflict implicit in space communications, that asociated with the ubiquitous national security activities. Conflicting claims will arise if states assert a right to use, or merely use, space communications systems for "illicit" activities or for activities with which international law simply does not deal. These might include jamming another nation's ground transmissions, broadcasting of propaganda directly into home receivers when this becomes feasible, or the like.

The Soviet Union has already suggested a rule barring the propagation of "national or racial hatred or enmity between nations." Such rules are easy to propose, but like the terms aggression, self-determination, peaceful coexistence and even "freedom of the press," they are difficult to define and make specific. They are convenient for the Soviet Union which will define or redefine them at will; satisfactory to the small states which can piously pronounce and ignore them; and awkward for those states which feel that law should have specific content so that it can be obeyed. It is often those states which really intend to be bound and whose standards, often, on the whole, surpass not only those of the others, but those of the empty rules which find the discussions embarrassingly hypocritical and the "rules" an unnecessary intrusion and perhaps dangerous since they will, in effect, be unilaterally bound. Perhaps this Russian proposal, in a field where they have made their mark as jammers of transmissions and broadcasters of propaganda, should be accepted by the United States in a gaming move of its own, while harping on existing Soviet practices. On the whole though, it might prove dangerous to accept rules which appear to be offered and espoused as part of the Marxist acceptance of expediency as a tool of international diplomacy and a part of socialist international law, the claim, in effect, that what the Socialist countries do in space as elsewhere is inevitably correct and in accordance with law.

c) *Meteorological and Navigation Systems*

Meteorological and navigation systems present fewer domestic and international areas of conflicting claims since they are not generally regarded as profit yielding activities. There is therefore no demand in the United States, for example, that these be anything but government systems. Nations clearly claim the right to establish such systems and other nations have not rejected these claims in principle though both systems always have potential military utility. Interestingly, despite Soviet protests as to the observation potentials of meteorological satellites, meteorology is one of the fields in which limited Soviet-American cooperative ventures are already planned.

The implications seem clear. The fact that navigation satellites can guide Polaris submarines as well as commercial planes and ships and that meteorological systems may "see" the earth and yield weather data useful for military as well as peaceful purposes serves to underscore the fact that legally and operationally any attempt to define and cordon off "peaceful" or "non-military" uses must ultimately rely on some arbitrary dividing concept, perhaps that of peacetime utility. In this case, there are significant, relatively inexpensive, economically valuable, desirable, humanitarian peacetime uses of these activities, ranging from aid to agriculture to rescue at sea, which make them worth doing. In wartime no doubt, attempts to interfere with the functioning of these systems would be considered reasonable self-defense.

d) *Observation Satellites*

This brings us to the closely related but much more volatile question of using space to observe earth activities. Even here, observation can be roughly divided into peaceful uses, both for gaining scientific knowledge and peacekeeping, and more direct military uses. Scientists want to observe the earth to gain more basic knowledge of its size, shape and physical characteristics, for meteorological purposes, as noted, and the like. Many of these observations, it is true, however innocent, may give information, even if inadvertently, on states and thus cannot avoid violating the "sanctity" of their national territory.

National peacekeeping systems, such as the proposed American early warning systems against surprise attack have led to conflicts of definition and interpretation of their true purposes. In this thermo-nuclear rocket age, the United States has insisted that a right to know of warlike preparations within a closed society like the Soviet Union is essential to the security and even the survival of the free world and is therefore a legal right. Since in the United States view these systems are defensive only, they are justified even under the U.N. Charter, wherever placed. To this, Russia has objected on the grounds that since she will in fact never launch an aggression, any such system must itself be designed in reality for attack purposes and is itself aggressive. Morover, in any event, Russia rejects the "use of artificial satellites for the collection of intelligence information in the territory" of a state as, under all circumstances, espionage and illegal wherever conducted. This latter crucial concept is certainly not clear in international law and may well not be at all applicable to many types of national peacekeeping warning systems. Those, for example, which collect data on incoming missiles from outside the potential aggressor's territory, however defined, would seem clearly more in the nature of self-defense than espionage activities. Like so many lines of course, the conceptual division is by nature arbitrary and the law is never precise in the borderline case.

It would seem that, however traumatic, sincere peace-loving states can be expected to accept the general legality of essential peacekeeping activities in space and elsewhere especially since it can be predicted that, when involved, all states will insist on their right to self-defense. The issues which are open to debate, to intellectual conflict, are therefore both conceptual, definitional and organizational. They involve which elements of information gathering can be included as peacekeeping, which are "essential" in different likely circumstances, and who should perform them in each case.

At one extreme, a universal arms control and inspection system, using satellites, would be legal and its information-gathering activities could not constitute espionage. Indeed one of the most productive peaceful uses of space may well be information-gathering for peace preservation, whether the systems are nationally or internationally directed. Unfortunately, we cannot objectively measure the intentions of nations; we cannot easily devise methods of refuting an allegation that information is being gathered in good faith solely in an effort to keep the peace. Worse yet, information useful for this purpose is also useful if peace is lost. This has never, and cannot, stop nations from collecting such information as they need to keep the peace or to preserve their existence in wartime and, hence, this cannot under all circumstances be held to be internationally illegal.

There is thus a possible, admittedly arbitrary, distinction that one can make. Space activities which are very productive in peacetime, meteorological and navigation systems, for example, can be usefully considered basically peaceful space activities even if there is also a military or observation potential. The category would also include information-gathering of the stabilizing, peacekeeping type. Since in a general war, no obligations which conflict fundamentally with survival will be uniformly honored, other rules would in such a case have to apply. For a limited war, in so far as peacekeeping activities, which would become more important than ever, are to be pursued, an international administration of information-gathering activities might be especially creative.

Our third category of observation systems, those used specifically for targeting and other military fact-finding missions have also been claimed as legal by the United States. To the right of self-defense, there is added the additional claim that their location in outer space, outside the territorial sovereignty of any state, permits their characterization as legal. This represents an implied support to the illegality of such surveillance elsewhere, notably in national air space, which the United States still continues to support in some parts of the globe, a tactical and legal position one could question, but not here. Such surveillance activities in space are characterized as military but defensive and hence not aggressive and do not, in the American view, in any sense run afoul of the principles of the United Nations Charter. It is equated with observation from the "free" high seas, or "free" air space or from friendly countries which we consider permissible in law. Here too the Soviet Union takes exception. Observation for any non-aggressive purpose from outer space is then permissible in the American view and, indeed, at least at one time Secretary Quarles asserted that the United States would not object to

Soviet surveillance satellites. It is not permissible in the Russian view which in turn claims that it is espionage and that espionage (though universally practiced) is an international wrong, constituting interference in a state's internal affairs and is hence illegal both under general and Charter law. There is thus at present an important political conflict over claimed legal rights to utilize some of the most important potentials of space. It is a political conflict if for no other reason than that on these matters in space the applicable law has yet to be made and formalized, perhaps after space is defined for these purposes.

CLAIMS RELATING TO RECOGNIZED MILITARY USES OF OUTER SPACE

In addition to the military uses we have already met, space is being used for other, near in, more clearly military purposes. Nations with ICBM capabilities have tested and presumably will continue to test these systems. As already suggested, under most present definitions this involves at least a brief passage through outer space. There do not appear to have been protests about or conflict over the space traverse of these weapons undergoing testing. It would be difficult now to keep others from testing similar products. At least the testing of "conventional" weapons must therefore at present be considered an acceptable "peaceful" use.

Next, we may encounter claims to orbit space weapons systems or military space stations. As far as we know, no nation has thus far orbited weapons. Both the United States and the Soviet Union over the years suggested an agreed ban on such an activity, indicating perhaps that, absent a specific ban, this use can no more be classed as illegal even under a regime of charter-limited "peaceful" uses than could the existence of national fleets on the seas, military aircraft with atomic bombs over the nation or over the seas, submarines under the high seas or missile sites on one's own or on friendly territory. In 1963, the United Nations General Assembly recommended that weapons of mass destruction not be orbited but even though Russia and the United States, not needing these systems now, have thus agreed on a ban, it is quite possible that smaller space powers for whom they would be far more valuable, and other emerging major powers, wishing to catch up fast, or even the present great powers at a later date when one of the new groups emerges as a threat, may claim anew the right to orbit nuclear weapons as "equalizers." This might, of course, be done in secret without the assertion of claims.

Another set of issues involves the right to test nuclear devices at high altitudes and in deep space. Both space powers have conducted such tests. They do interfere with scientific observation, ground communications, natural phenomena and the like, thus competing with other claims to a free use of space. Though the facts are unclear they may also have some effects on health through fallout, thus leading to a claim on behalf of all men to an undistorted survival. This last claim, the right of man to survive even against the claimed right of the nations to defend themselves, is in our world the hardest of all to specify operationally and to promote. Who speaks for man?

There were again official suggestions for a ban on space tests over several years as well as Soviet threats of hidden tests perhaps, to taunt the United States, on the other side of the moon. The partial nuclear test ban treaty of 1963 includes outer space as a place "off limits" to testing. Without this agreed ban, it does not now seem that the Charter or the 1961 Resolution made testing illegal in any accepted sense. Unless the ban becomes universal, as is unlikely in the short run at least, there presumably will eventually be claims by other states to try this facet of military experimentation and preparedness when they acquire the capability.

CLAIMS RELATING TO THE EXTENSION OF SOVEREIGNTY INTO SPACE

Turning to the more direct extension of sovereignty into space, there are at least three categories of claims states have made or could make. First, there is already a consensus that states retain sovereignty in and to the vehicles and personnel they send into outer space. East and West agree in principle but difficulties remain. It seems likely that potential conflicts in this area will be resolved through "return-to-earth" agreements and arrangements by which states acknowledge their responsibility for incidents involving their space vehicles as to damage, liability and the like, though Soviet treatment of aerial intruders in the past, particularly by the U-2 plane and pilot, prevent undue optimism in practice.

Second, there are potential claims to sovereignty in space above the airspace in which states are now sovereign. "Air space" remains undefined. Claims to sovereignty in space seem unlikely, due to the physical facts except perhaps for the atmosphere, and for two additional reasons. First, a state clearly has the legal ability to defend itself wherever a peril exists. Due to the nature of space activities, claims to areas would be difficult to defend in fact, and might contribute little more to national defense than does the general right to defend against hostile acts or devices, wherever located. Second, the unanimous U.N. Resolution of December 20, 1961 commends to states the principle that "Outer space and celestial bodies . . . are not subject to national appropriation. . . ." It would be awkward for any state to dispute this projected principle, though the possibility cannot be discounted if some important national gain would result.

Third, states may claim a right to exercise sovereignty over celestial bodies or at least control over bases on celestial bodies. The U.N. Resolution just mentioned and repeated statements of Russian, American and other national spokesmen reject this claim in the interests of use by all. There is nevertheless, always the possibility of exclusionary acts without a formal claim to sovereignty if some areas prove especially rich or suitable for military activities or populations. The U.N. proposed rule is negative. It does not provide an alternative regime to national claims nor channel or control conceivable future claims to economic prestige or even military rights in competition with other states.

CLAIMS IN SUMMARY

Looking at the range of conflict over claims it thus appears that the potentially most deadly are the claims of nation against nation. These may be for free access, or fair access to space itself on the part of smaller nations, cramped for launching room, and to space resources as against claims to exclusive use. They may be for self-defense, including warning against surprise attack and a "right to know" of a potential enemy's activities, as against a claim to national secrecy which is itself a part of self-defense. They may be for the use of resources for development of the poor nations on earth as contrasted with hurling resources into space.

A second group of claims is that of economic and professional interest groups within and across nations. Which projects will receive preference? What decision making institutions exist to choose between alternative space projects which for financial or scientific reasons may be mutually exclusive. Which groups will operate the space facilities decided on? For whose gain? On whose performance standards? With what systems of control or regulation?

Broadly speaking these all also may involve the claims of man as against self-seeking national states—the right to survival, to avoid genetic distortion, to freedom from starvation. Human goals conflict and hence imply the necessity for compromise and for institutions to effect and make effective the agreed divisions. We are left with the problem of furthering man's goals in space in a conceptually, emotionally and power divided world. Can this be done by self-denying, unpoliced UN resolutions or treaties, or by a space mechanism, a space regime alone? Does it require an institutionalized world order which flows into and controls space activities as well?

III THE RESOLUTION OF CONFLICTING CLAIMS

If anything is clear it is that the range of actual and potential claims to use outer space is broad and, in a substantial degree, bound up with national prestige and security considerations. How are important claims resolved within a nation and between nations?

Using the United States, an individualistic democracy, as one of many possible existing models, it is apparent that the framework of organized government offers the possibility for resolution of most major controversies through the use of power without the resort to violence. The Executive and Congress respond to the private and public pressures most forcefully presented, and base their judgment on what seems the best possible compromise within, in Theodore Sorenson's words, "the limits of available resources, . . . available time . . . previous commitments . . . available information . . . and the laws of the land." In this way it was decided to create NASA to carry forward basic space programs, and to create a particular form of a satellite communications system, for example. Here, opposition was diffuse; the consumer has little understanding and few ardent advocates. The Executive and Congress similarly allocate government resources between military and scientific claims and programs, again responding to pressures, information, views as to goals and the like. The Executive, aided by scientific advisers and committees, largely allocates resources between scientific programs based on evaluation of prestige potential, success potential, time, and so on. Administrative agencies, such as the Federal Communicatons Commission, make allocations between scientific, communications and other claims for frequencies and other valuable resources. All of these decisions are made of course, against a background of lobbying, of the use of power, prestige, influence, authority, money, electioneering, log-rolling, fireside chats and press conferences, the Departments of State and Defense, of mysterious submarines off the coast at the time of hearings on naval appropriations. Even to attempt to list what goes into a democratic decision shows a circus of competing hopes, aspirations, conviction, greed, pride, personal ambition—the list is endless. Of course from the point of view of decision-making theory, a more rational national government than that of the United States or of any existing government could be designed but there it is.

Moreover, it provides the legal, political framework within which even difficult conflicts over the use of exclusive resources can be adjusted and the resolution carried out. This may also be by courts if no one group can marshal enough power in Congress or the Executive or if some person or segment of the public is denied a claim fairly made under the law. Even the waters of the Colorado, if not of the Jordan, can be divided peacefully. In a sense, the existence of a solution-giving and enforcing mechanism is more important than its equity or conformity with some abstract notions of individual preference or justice. As Lord Mansfield said of the commercial law a century ago, it is often most important to have a stable, understood legal situation. Behaviour can then be adapted to it to make the best of it. Arizona may use the Colorado's waters less fruitfully than California but they will be fruitfully used. The same is true of off-shore oil and a space communications system. American decision-making could be improved but the vital thing is that it exists and functions without general warfare if also without achieving perfect equity.

Internationally, decision-making is decentralized and institutions of comparable stature for reaching solutions, enforcing them, and forcefully channeling conflicting pressures and claims into non-violent patterns of accommodation are largely lacking. As the specific "legal" framework for resolving conflicting claims to use outer space, we find U.N. resolutions which commend to states the principles that international law extends to space activities, that national sovereignty shall not be extended there and that weapons of mass destruction not be orbitted. There is a ban on nuclear explosions in outer space. There are also statements by national leaders approving a concept of free, peaceful use of outer space, but reserving essential national positions. There are assertions by scholars that to the extent nations have not protested satellite over-flights, there may be a rule of customary international law that, like the high seas, outer space is already legally available for the peaceful commerce of all. Of course states have not as yet developed the ability to interfere with these overflights as some, at least, can with flights of a U-2, which, incidentally, also went officially unprotested for some years.

There are also some international institutions already in existence which will help to resolve some of the important but not militarily crucial competing claims. Claims between groups of scientists for priorities can in part be evaluated through COSPAR, the international scientific unions and through informal consultations between scientists of different nations. Provision for sterilization of space craft has been discussed, for example, in CETEX during the IGY and now in COSPAR. The United States has used these techniques in conection with Project West Ford and some of the high altitude tests and has suggested a more extensive use of COSPAR's apparatus. It seems clear though that such consultations will not override defense claims. The United States has rejected as a "veto" device Soviet proposals for "prior discussion of and agreement upon" *any* measures undertaken in space which might in an undefined way hinder the use of space for peaceful purposes.

The ITU, similarly, has dealt with and will continue to deal with the claims of scientists, communications systems and all others needing radio frequencies and is charged with making allocations of these scarce, valuable rights. The U.N.'s General Assembly and its Outer Space Committee may be able to suggest useful principles, or begin the process of treaty formulation, in questions of nationality of space vehicles, liability and return-to-earth covenants.

The great gap in the decentralized international community is found, of course, in just those remaining areas which are security-suffused. Where is the legal-political framework which will provide for a peaceful decision between the American claim of a right to know in a nuclear-missile age and the Soviet claim of a right to inviolable secrecy? The record of resolution of this type of security-suffused conflict in our own disorderly world community is extremely poor to date. To a state, as Dean Acheson said on April 27, 1963, "the survival of states is above law—it must be."

Nationally, many basic conflicts of interest are settled by executive or legislative decision, by a form of imposed, negotiated compromise between competing power groups. Sometimes the courts, as with the Colorado River, are also involved. Each group aims for a social decision by the organ, executive, legislative or judicial, where, considering its power base, it is most favored. But the decision is made within an agreed, orderly framework by the maximum use of power perhaps but not of force. It is certainly not premature to suggest that international accommodation in militarily significant problems, including many of the claims to use outer space, can probably only be achieved within a structured, governmental framework as well.

Of course, an effective world structure might well dampen and even reverse the race into space itself, if on a world basis, after the elimination of the necessity to pursue national prestige and power, other competing fields of concentrated human intellectual effort and capital investment seemed more desirable. After all the whole field of space endeavors must ultimately compete for resources with other possible investment programs. The status of its competitive position would no doubt be modified in a well-organized international community. Indeed this is merely the converse of the earlier observation that mankind's enormous assault on space, with the problems of survival and conflict that accompany it, was and is at root a strategic and national prestige venture.

8

E. R. Platig

THE FUTURE:
COMMENTS AND QUERIES

In the early 1960's we live so close to the advent of the space age that fascination is more characteristic of our response than is reflection. It may even be that in the initial flush of fascination we have erred in a way reminiscent of the rashness with which we misnamed the nuclear age the atomic age. The real space age may be far ahead of us—the age opened by Sputnik I may be more accurately thought of as the age of earth satellites. To be sure, there have been some spectacular probes of far space, but in essence these provide only more sophisticated observations of an environment that has stimulated man's curiosity ever since he first cast an eye heavenward.

As the papers in this volume make clear, the more immediately significant "space events" of the past few years—and probably of many years to come—are those that have demonstrated the feasibility of girdling the globe on which we live with satellites for communication, observational and meteorological uses and, therefore, of economic, social and military importance for the life of man on earth. However much we may be fascinated by the spectacular idea of putting a man on the moon, we ought not to overlook the fact that the moon is only the oldest of the earth's satellites. It is perhaps not too rash to suggest that before man's venturing beyond the moon to the outer reaches of space takes on significant proportions, the social organization of the planet from which he starts may be much changed—partly because of the age of earth satellites.

So mundane is the current "space age" that it is still possible to speak separately of its impact upon domestic and international affairs. The earth satellites may well serve to further deprive this distinction of its fading validity, but for the time being it is still useful.

SPACE AND HOMO SAPIENS

Those space activities that most nearly succeed in overarching the domestic-international distinction are the pure scientific ones. These activities seem most clearly to have implications for man as man as well as for man as national. Thus when Robert Jastrow suggests some of the things we can expect to learn about the structure and origin of the universe and the dynamics of the atmosphere, we have a heightened sense of the world-wide validity of basic knowledge as one of the hallmarks of the modern era. But this global community of science and scientific knowledge, as Howard J. Taubenfeld suggests, is not free of internal conflicts. Furthermore, the global community of science is intermingled with the society of states which in turn is rent by rivalries of power and purpose so that states use science as both an instrument of their rivalries and a measure of their power. Though touching upon some aspects of them, the papers in this volume leave for others the difficult task of exploring the subtle relations that exist and might exist among: national scientific capabilities; the programs, organizations and aspirations of international science; and the organization, ethos and practice of international politics. Those who believe that learning and the arts are favored by conditions of peace and harmony may want to ponder the significance of Taubenfeld's provocative observation that in a different world political system, space science might well find itself in a less favorable competitive position vis-a-vis other demands upon manpower and resources.

Jastrow is hopeful that the new scientific knowledge gained from space exploration will affect the very vitals of human thought in a manner similar to that of the great age of discovery. This too is a matter that deserves more attention. One might ask how soon and to what extent space exploration is likely to change the basic orientation of man to the universe. Is it likely that the modern world view will be more profoundly affected by developments in molecular biology or by those in space? One can hope that at least some philosophers are searching for the larger significance of scientific advances and seeking to incorporate them into man's understanding of himself and his world. Even more, one can hope that theologians will keep close enough to the cutting edge of science that new knowledge can serve to heighten our sense and expand our understanding of that which is eternal and unchanging. These are not tasks assayed in this brief book, but philosophers and theologians—especially those interested in the social consequences of scientific change—will find here some interesting grist for their mills.

SPACE AND DOMESTIC AFFAIRS

The Cost of Science:

As Leonard S. Silk makes clear, we in the United States have entered an era when some difficult choices have to be made concerning the allocation of manpower and resources to different fields of scientific endeavor. These choices are forced upon us not just by the space program but also because science and research have increasingly become a significant part of any large enterprise. Whether research is thought of as merely gathering and organizing existing knowledge so it can be applied to the achievement of specific objectives, or whether it is thought of as inquiry directed toward filling certain lacunae in our basic knowledge that impair our ability to achieve desired objectives, or whether it is thought of as basic inquiry directed primarily by the scientist's "feel" for his subject, its demands upon the budget of any undertaking are insistent and difficult to deny. These demands reflect both the complex infrastructure of modern science (science information handling alone is on the verge of being a big business) and the intricacy and power of the research tools needed to push back the frontiers of knowledge. Because these demands are increasingly made upon public funds, they come increasingly under a judgment that is more social and political than scientific.

As a society we face some difficult problems as to which dimensions of these socio-scientific judgments should be left to the discretion of scientists (and how in those cases society is to monitor their judgments in order to minimize the intrusion of non-scientific criteria) and which dimensions fall in the purview of others. It is unlikely that we will be able to resolve questions of this type unless we first develop a better analysis of the problems. Current analysis is cursed by sloppy conceptualization that tempts us to treat as one item in the federal budget the 15 billion dollars for so-called Research and Development. We badly need some restructuring of our thought to permit us to distinguish self-directed basic research, stimulated basic research, programmatic basic research, applied research, development, technology and engineering— and to allocate costs to the facilities, processes and manpower appropriate to each. Without such reconceptualization, the needs of science are liable to be obscured by the needs of large social purposes and the criteria for making socio-scientific choices are liable to give either too little or too much weight to the intrinsic nature and merits of fundamental scientific research. It is this large problem of harnessing science to society, of deriving social benefit from science without destroying the integrity of science, that accounts for much of the emotion generated by space appropriations and programs. Mr. Silk does well to call our attention to the problem—we will neglect it at our peril.

Science and the Policy Process:

Because the natural sciences and their related technologies do play such an important part in public programs, and because policy choices that integrate scientific and political judgments must be made, our age is also plagued by questions concerning the role of the scientist in policy matters and the scientific knowledge needed by policy makers who are not scientists. Robert Jastrow is highly critical of his fellow scientists for perpetuating through their "intellectual arrogance" what he calls the "myth of scientific truth and infallibility." He clearly does not share the view held by some scientists that, by the nature of their method, scientists are better able than others to solve social problems. But even when scientists accept a more limited definition of their role—as an increasing proportion of them seem to be doing —difficult questions remain as to how and at what points scientific considerations should be fed into the policy making process. Jastrow's suggestions tend toward the conclusion that the best answers to these questions can be had only when the non-scientist policy maker has developed "a minimal knowledge of science so that he can make critical judgments on the basis of an understanding of all the forces, including that of science, which are at work in society." The argument thus comes full circle and we are made aware that the problem of providing adequate science education for the non-scientist has also been exacerbated by the space age.

This is a problem that must be faced at almost all age levels in our population; it has been receiving imaginative treatment as it manifests itself at the primary and secondary school levels. More recently the science curriculum of the liberal arts college has been coming under review and Jastrow has a suggestion appropriate for that level. What has yet to be done on a scale adequate to the seriousness of the need, is the modernization and revitalization of the scientific knowledge and understanding of those individuals now in policy positions whose science education, even if not sadly

neglected, ended 15 or 25 years ago and is now obsolete,
C. P. Snow is no doubt correct that "there is no excuse for
letting another generation be as vastly ignorant or as devoid
of understanding and sympathy, as we are ourselves." But we
are in for some very difficult years during this generation
unless suitable steps are taken to overcome the ignorance and
indifference of those policy makers who—for good or ill—
will decide both how society adjusts to the impact of scientific
advance and how society moves to stimulate or stifle scientific
advance. The seriousness of this problem is pointed up by
Silk's discussion of the deficiencies in the scientific education
of engineers graduated prior to 1950. "Continuing education"
is rapidly becoming in our society a vital necessity rather than
an adult leisure time activity.

Space and the Political Economy:

Calculating the costs of science, sorting out the scientific
dimensions of larger programs, and adjusting the policy process to the need for scientific expertise may strike many
readers as highly abstract problems. Much less abstract are
the effects a multi-billion dollar space program is having
upon the economy and society of the United States. Silk
reviews for us some of the more direct effects in the form
of technological innovations of importance to the civilian
economy and in the form of manpower requirements. He is
not optimistic that the space program can pay its way by
supplying technological innovation to the national economy.
As for manpower, Silk's analysis suggests that the space program both breeds and consumes highly trained manpower.
He does not attempt to provide us with the social calculus
by means of which we can judge the net value of these contradictory processes. The elements of the calculus are made
more complex when one notes that space age facilities and
NASA support to university programs have their impacts
in some regions of the country that otherwise would have
little incentive to enter an advanced stage of science and
technology. Nor can one ignore the political considerations

that both influence the selection of sites for space age facilities and are influenced by NASA-induced changes in the socio-economic structure of certain regions.

At another level, Silk points to the new modes of government-industry relations that are emerging out of this program of large public expenditure. Some of these new modes were already in evidence prior to the space age—for example, the negotiated, cost-reimbursement contract and the non-governmental, non-profit research organization that depends upon government contracts and grants. So far the major institutional innovation of the space age is the new Communications Satellite Corporation which, as Horace P. Moulton and Howard J. Taubenfeld as well as Silk indicate, is a peculiar animal indeed. Given the fact that the foreign and international business negotiations of this profit-making corporation are by law to be conducted within the framework of relevant foreign policy considerations as specified by the Department of State, one has an enhanced sense of the difficulty of drawing the line between the private and public sectors of American society.

What we see here are some specific examples of larger developments that have yet to be adequately analysed. In part, these are developments we often obscure in the vague term "mixed economy." Clearly American social and economic practice has outrun its doctrine. While this may be testimony to the wisdom of our pragmatic approach to social matters, we might do well to pay more attention to the doctrinal implications of some of our practices to be sure that they do not lead us to ends we would just as soon avoid. This is true not only of government-industry relations but also of government-university relations; we have not only a mixed economy but also a much more varied mix of intellectual instititions whose genesis and dynamics are still poorly understood. This point is given poignancy by David E. Lilienthal's suggestion in a recent book entitled *Change, Hope and the Bomb*, that we consider new teaching institutions to replace those older universities that have become so deeply involved in sponsored research programs. It is perhaps worth stressing once more that impetus has been given these developments by the national space program, but their roots are deeply embedded in all the mushrooming scientific and technological complexities of the post-war era.

Our understanding of the impact of space programs upon American society would be furthered were we to have at hand some comparative data and analyses. What internal changes in the Soviet Union are attributable in whole or in significant part to Soviet space programs? What about the United Kingdom? Japan? France? And, perhaps most interesting for students of political integration, what impact will the burgeoning space plans of Western Europe have upon the affairs of a region in which the domestic-international distinction is increasingly difficult to maintain?

SPACE AND THE RELATIONS OF NATIONS

Three papers (Woetzel, Falk and Taubenfeld) address themselves directly to the international political and legal aspects of space. They either assume or argue that much of the motivation for the programs of the space powers is to be found in their rivalry for power and prestige. Taubenfeld puts it most succinctly: "The costly race into space is engined by the belief, perhaps erroneous, that not only national prestige but, somehow, national survival may be at stake."

The most high-powered fuel driving this engine of belief is distilled from the direct military uses and militarily significant uses of space. Woetzel provides us with a brief rundown of space weapons systems. But neither he nor anyone else seems overly concerned that space might soon be turned into an arena for military activity or a staging area for military assaults upon the earth. The most horrendous sounding of the immediately available space weapons—a nuclear bomb in orbit—does not appear to be a weapon of great attraction for those states with the greatest capability for developing it. There are grave questions concerning its accuracy, costs, size limitations, accident proneness, vulnerability and capacity for surprise. Apparently the most that can be said for the United States orbiting such weapons and otherwise arming space is that it might put additional pressure upon the Soviets to enter into arms control agreements. This, however, is an argument that cuts both ways. In addition there is the possibility —one cannot predict the probability—that one of the space powers might seek a psychological advantage by deploying nuclear weapons in space. For the time being, however, the superpowers have agreed that space should be used for peaceful purposes and though, as Woetzel makes clear, some important ambiguities remain, the agreement may indicate that through individual assessments they have arrived at a common conclusion concerning the difficulties of using space for direct military purposes.

Whatever specific military uses might be made of space in the future, it is instructive to note that forseeable uses do not create for the relations of states new problems that are in essence different from the existing problems posed by military force in the nuclear age. Woetzel's discussion leads to the conclusion that questions about the legality of the use and the threat of force in or from space are not different in kind from those same questions on the earth. His resume reveals that the substance of arguments concerning the extent of the right of self-defense under the United Nations Charter is little affected by space factors. Similarly his analysis of the problems of arms control suggests that their essence is little changed whether one is concerned with earthbound or space weapons systems.

The more immediate and interesting questions arise in connection with the possible military significance of observational satellites. There seems little doubt that some satellites now in operation yield militarily useful information to the observing state. Woetzel, Falk and Taubenfeld all treat of this matter, each with a slightly different emphasis and tone which the reader will have noted with interest. However, the most profound issue involving the relations of nations arises only indirectly out of the assumptions made by the various authors about the nature of international politics and law.

This issue is most clearly seen, though it is not joined, in the papers by Moulton and Falk. Underlying Moulton's treatment of commercial space communications is a highly pragmatic, positivist approach to international law. He emphasizes the way in which law grows out of precedent and out of specifiic cooperative ventures based upon common interest. His paper displays less concern for the overall shape of the law than for the adequacy of the specific framework it provides for getting on with the day-to-day work of the world. Falk, on the other hand, though he too pays homage to the tradition and practice of legal positivism, is not fully comfortable with it and would like to see the nations consider the requirements of "world order" as well as the requirements of their own interests before they move ahead with acts that may be precedent-setting. Out of consideration for the requirements of "world order" he counsels a higher degree of American self-restraint in the launching of surveillance satellite systems than does either Woetzel or Taubenfeld. Mr. Falk's argument is subtle and sophisticated—it deserves careful attention. But one wonders if his strong and understandable desire to encourage nations to sacrifice immediate and non-vital advantage for the general good does not lead him to gloss over the difficulties that lurk within the innocent concept of "world order." He fails to define—and therefore to distinguish from one another—the kind of "world order" to which he would like to have the United States commit itself and the kind of "world order" to which he believes there is a "minimum Soviet commitment." If there are no significant distinguishing features, then Falk's argument carries greater conviction. If, on the contrary, the nature of the future "world order" is one of the key objects of

U.S.-U.S.S.R. rivalry, then the wisdom of a policy of American self-denial in these matters is more questionable.

It is the opinion of Falk, and also of Woetzel, that American military surveillance of the Soviet Union from space is destabilizing in its effects upon the military relations of the U.S. and the U.S.S.R. However, on the basis of certain assumptions about the motivations of Soviet policy and the kind of world Soviet leaders seek, one can argue that American surveillance satellites serve a defensive, peace-keeping and stabilizing purpose. This is, in fact, the official American position which both Woetzel and Taubenfeld recapitulate, the latter apparently being more comfortable with it than the former. There is, however, a slightly different direction this argument can take which brings it more in line with Falk's concern for "world order" and at the same time avoids some of the ideological overtones of the official American position. It can be argued that American self-restraint serves better to build the foundations of a cooperative multi-national world if it becomes operative at a point different from that suggested by Falk. Instead of refusing to orbit survelliance statellites it may be more important for the United States to demonstrate to the Soviet Union that, even with the improved targeting information and other military advantages it derives from these satellites, its concern for "world order" and for avoiding nuclear devastation is so great that it will not make aggressive use of these advantages. One might even argue that the recent softening of the Soviet position on the question of observational satellites as well as other indications of Soviet "reasonableness" reflect appreciation of this American restraint.

It should be noted that not all space-connected rivalries for power and prestige are destined to take place between the United States and the Soviet Union. It is difficult at the moment to foresee specifically what other rivalries might emerge, but there are ample indications in the papers by Silk, Taubenfeld and Moulton that space communications provide a potential field of intense rivalry within the Atlantic Community. Those interested in bulding the foundations of the Atlantic Community might well look to this area of space activity to see how it might serve rather than hamper their purposes. Unless great care is exercised in the next few years, history may judge that the "regional order" in the Atlantic area was ill-served by the haste with which the United States moved to capture the lead in commercial space communications.

Finally, no book published in the mid-1960's and dealing with space affairs would be complete without some mention of the Peoples Republic of China. It is not inconceivable that the Communist Chinese may see in space an opportunity for a new and more impressive "great leap forward." One can imagine both technological and psychological reasons why the Chinese might give to the development of a space capability—however primitive—a higher priority than a nuclear capability. Should the Chinese find such reasons persuasive, it would be well that American opinion and policy not be taken by surprise.

As man expands his control over the physical forces that hold him to earth and pursues the implications, many other problems will unfold for his life in society. The shape of that life may well be changed quite drastically; even the quality may be affected in important ways. But the basic quality of human life—the extent to which it is just, peaceful and creative (qualities, it is sometimes necessary to add, that differ from affluence, affability and productivity, respectively)— will continue to be dependent more upon the humility with which man recognizes his limitations than upon the pride with which he views his works.